May 9, 1970

To John Auer.

a loyal friend who
embodies so many
of the good ideas
in this book.

Gratefully,
Joe Gallagher

The Christian Under Pressure

The Christian Under Pressure

Joseph Gallagher

Ave Maria Press
Notre Dame, Indiana 46556

Nihil Obstat:
John L. Reedy, C.S.C.
Censor Deputatus

Imprimatur:
✠Most Rev. Leo A. Pursley, D.D.
Bishop of Fort Wayne-South Bend

Library of Congress Catalog Card No: 76-105099

To my Alma Mater of 1951

Baltimore's

Old St. Mary's Seminary (1791-1969)

where caring was curing.

Your walls sheltered me,

your beautiful people re-created me

during your two final years.

Your best wine was last.

Contents

Gentleness

Though the late-looming moon can overtake
the black of night commandingly enough,
it wields even then a quiet, courteous splendor.
At times it comes most humbly yet,
while day prevails and the sun's loud glare
still trumpets shape and color forth from things.
Although its charms are palest then,
as overshadowed by a fiercer presence,
the modest moon seems mindless of itself
and pleased enough to gaze unnoticed
upon a world it never made—
like the cherubs (marginal, superfluous)
who study selflessly Raffaello's study
of Madonna and her child.

While this moon, then, has often seen
the ways of sun upon the earth,
the sun has never yet
in all its circling, all its searching ages
known the grace of moonlit night,
has yet to feel the muted sorcery of moon
upon a cloud in drift or crusted snow,
upon a stirred tree's pallid, liquid leaves,
or some tumbling, gleam-stocked stream.

Which may suggest that something
can be said in this wild
world for gentleness
and being
less.

A boy remains a boy until there is need for a man. So it is that the pressures of need, of timeliness, of opportunity cause many precious qualities to be born, to grow and to blossom.

1

The Pressurized Christian

JUST BEFORE their epoch-making walk on the moon, astronauts Armstrong and Aldrin performed a functional act: They lowered the pressure in their spaceship. But it was also a symbolic act. Their astonishing journey was full of risks, to be sure; and many earthlings were unnerved about the disaster which could have occurred.

But the earth itself is a spaceship—an increasingly pressurized one. And for a brief spell, the brooding pressure of earthly life was somehow lightened by the gallantly human and supremely successful adventure of the spacemen.

For a brief space, humanity as a whole seemed to become one closely knit family raising its thoughts and its eyes upward from the conflict-ridden and dispiriting earth. Hangdog man, drooping with world weariness, was once again what the ancient Greeks named him— *"anthropos":* the animal with "upturned face," as the very word *anthropos* is said to mean.

At that moment, in July of 1969 A.D., a humanity which appears to have lost its way found its way to the moon in the person of two valiant men. Everyone seemed to be watching together and pulling together for the men on the moon. The triumph was everyone's triumph. Here at last was an achievement which everyone could enjoy, even those who felt that the money involved would have been better spent for projects 240,000 miles closer to the earth. The cleansing and tonic emotions of amazement, admiration and thankfulness washed over the spirit of man and served to remind every man of his kinship with his fellow travelers on the spaceship called earth.

For Americans the moon trip, from blastoff over the Atlantic to splashdown in the Pacific, provided a sorely needed boost in national morale. After a prolonged season of war, assassinations, riots and other depressions, here at last was something American which could have gone wrong, but didn't go wrong. With so much bad news behind them, many Americans had probably steeled themselves for another catastrophe, and had to pinch themselves out of a disbelief that things could have gone so smoothly.

Once back in their moon ship, the astronauts again "turned on the pressure." So also, with the delightfully distracting moon mission completed, Americans returned to the insistent pressures of everyday life in the final days of the shattering 60's.

Yet, pressure itself is not the problem. After all, the earthmen could survive on the stark and alien moon only because they had brought their own atmosphere with them in their spaceship and space suits. To say that they brought their own atmosphere is to say that they transported their own pressures with them—pressures designed to maintain and promote

14

the functioning of the astronauts as human beings.

Hence, pressure as such is not the problem of our pressurized times. The Aztecs had a saying: A boy remains a boy until there is need for a man. So it is that the pressures of need, of timeliness, of opportunity cause many precious qualities to be born, to grow and to blossom.

Gabriel Moran has stressed the fact that the mature person is not the person without pressure, but rather the person who knows how to live with the push and pull of opposite pressures in his life.

"By an adult attitude," he wrote in the *National Catholic Reporter,* "is meant an ability to live between sets of characteristics which seem to be contradictory. The adult is neither controlled nor spontaneous, neither dependent nor independent, neither strong nor weak. Neither does he shift abruptly from one set of characteristics to another. He is one who has achieved a stable synthesis of these qualities, though the synthesis is not without its own inner tension. The cause of this tension is the paradox of ambiguity that life itself presents. The adult has to be dependent in an independent way and independent in a dependent way."

If I were asked to put this line of thought in mathematical terms, I would say that maturity is not a *number,* but an *equation.* To be mature is not a matter of getting "100" in some kind of test. It is rather a balancing of forces so that A equals B equals C. A, B and C would represent the various ingredients of a healthy life which have to be integrated in a reasonably harmonious balance—such ingredients as self and others, passing goals and long-range values, bodily needs and claims of the spirit, intellect and emotion, action and receptivity, self-assertion and co-operation.

These ingredients have to be synthesized in a

15

flexible state allowing for some degree of rippling and shoving back and forth. It is this ability to hold and yet give under stress that marks the maturing person. On this score the comparison which suggests itself is the steel bridge which is so designed that it can safely expand and contract under varying weather conditions. But such an achievement will not and should not eliminate tension. For, as Carl Jung once remarked, the serious problems of life are never solved, and if they seem to have been solved, something humanly important has been lost.

Now, in any event and under all conditions, the supreme goal of any human being is to become human and to stay human—to be or to become what a man is, what a man is supposed to be. It is, of course, as easy as oil to make a statement like that, while it is in fact a lifelong task of each man and of humanity as a whole to find out just what it means to be human in any and all circumstances. For "man is always more than man," as the philosopher Blaise Pascal summed up the mystery of man's unique open-endedness.

But the pressure problem of so many people today is the problem of too-muchness. There is too much pressure, too many pressures, too many seemingly irreconcilable pressures. A growing paralysis and apathy of spirit appear to be resulting from an over-pressurized life of too much noise, too much news, too many options, too many distractions, too much haste, too many meetings, too many memos, too many traffic signs, too many social obligations, too many books to read, movies to see, magazines to scan, letters to answer, phone calls to make, pitfalls to be avoided, cautions to take.

If Shakespeare could wonder, "How with this rage shall beauty hold a plea?"; if Wordsworth could complain, "The world is too much with us / Getting and

16

spending we lay waste our powers," they should be alive today writing their sonnets—if they had the time. True, we have countless time-saving devices, but we seem to have less and less time to be human. We have marvelously enriched the field of communications, but many of us feel that it is harder than ever to communicate with other human beings. (In Gian Carlo Menotti's play, *The Telephone,* a man leaves his girlfriend's house in desperation and proposes to her over the telephone, since he keeps getting interrupted by phone calls made to the girl.)

Scholars tell us that the human race is undergoing profound social and cultural changes. What is especially new about the current transformations is the speed with which they are occurring, and the vast numbers of human beings who are involved in the change. For the wide earth has shrunken into a global village, thanks to the swiftness and everywhereness of radio, television and newspapers.

Men are creatures of habit, but history is demanding that they react to so many changes in so short a time, that habits have almost become emotional hindrances instead of helps. Some of our habits are like those solidly embedded guns of the Maginot Line which France aimed securely at Germany before World War II. Only, the German Army invaded France by the side door, and the fixed guns couldn't be turned that way. History is hitting our habits from the side, and we aren't prepared to grapple with events from that unexpected quarter.

Catholics have had a special measure of pressure to deal with. For many of them, the Church changes which followed Vatican II have been a matter of "too much too soon." A Jewish psychiatrist once said that he liked to treat Catholic patients because "they have metaphysical underpinnings" in their makeup.

Yet many Catholics today feel that the pins have been knocked out from under them by changes which they dislike, don't understand, and feel threatened by. Other Catholics, concerned with problems like world peace, overpopulation and racism are disappointed, angered and disaffected because the official Church has not made enough changes, nor made them fast enough.

(The Catholic confusion even antedates Vatican II. I remember giving a tour of Baltimore's new cathedral in 1960. One lady was disturbed to find Judas portrayed in a stained-glass window. Sensing her problem, I tried to explain, "That isn't to honor Judas. He is portrayed there because he was present at the Last Supper." "Oh," she answered with some relief, "I thought that maybe there had been some recent developments.")

So here we are, in the Church and out of it, a growing mass of uptight people, wrestling with our own hang-ups and those of the people around us. We have the gift of life. We sense (despite all our doubting) that it is a precious gift, full of promise, brimming with undeciphered glories. Yet, while we grow hard in some spots, and soft in others, we feel that we are not ripening. We feel that some secret has outwitted us, that some hostile fate is playing tricks with us. So, in the expressive words of the younger generation, many of us are "turned off" and we "drop out." We find ourselves growing cynical or apathetic.

A century ago (for "life after birth" was never an easy condition to sustain), Emily Dickinson sketched out the way a man's ardor and enthusiasm for life can weaken and decline:

> The heart asks pleasure first;
> And then, excuse from pain;
> And then, those little anodynes

18

That deaden suffering;
And then to go to sleep;
And then, if it should be
The will of its Inquisitor
The liberty to die.

This is a far cry from the vitality celebrated in a current folk song: "To be alive and feeling free, and to have everyone in your family; to be alive in every way, Oh how great it is, to be alive!"

I listen to young people singing this song and wonder how successful they will be, not in adding years to their life, but in the sterner task of adding life to their years. (How rightly Robert Louis Stevenson spoke of the great *task* of happiness.) Will they end up 10 or 20 years from now with the dreary impression that "life goes on forever like the gnawing of a mouse"?

It needn't be that way, and it shouldn't be. True, the passing of time and the accumulation of experiences will alter a person's notion of what "being alive" really means, and the sources and showings of satisfaction will not always have to be as immediate and bubbly as young people naturally incline to think they are.

But if we can learn how to fight creatively against the drift to dullness, if we can learn to accept the help of other people in that fight, we can avoid dying in our 20's and being buried in our 70's. There is no law saying that we have to become the lifeless sort of people spoken of in T. S. Eliot's play, *The Family Reunion:* "You are all people / To whom nothing has happened, at most a continual impact / Of external events."

I believe we can help one another enormously in this task of becoming and staying alive and human.

Life teaches something to every one of us, and we should share our humanity with one another much more than we do.

In an article in *America* magazine, Dr. James J. Diamond tells of a patient he once met. She had a numbered tattoo on her arm, an unfading reminder of her days in the Nazi concentration camp of Buchenwald. The doctor asked her if she would like to have the tattoo removed by surgery, but she said no. She said she would wear it to the grave, for it was her diploma from the school of life. Her words, as the doctor recalled them, were something like this: "Doctor, I don't know where you learned what life is, but I know where I learned it."

Sharing with others what we have learned from that school is one of the most humane things we can do. Last year a psychiatrist friend did just that for his children, who were all of about college age. He took time out from his busy life to write for them a statement of his philosophy of life. He told them, for instance, "As a physician, my work has revealed at the merely human level, the astonishing powers of personal love to create, heal and integrate." Elsewhere in his spiritual testament he stated, "All of my scientific search has convinced me that the universe is not absurd, but ordered beyond my wildest fantasy."

Here was a man who had practiced the art of healing for many decades, in this country and overseas, on the battlefield and in peacetime, in hospitals and private offices. He had much indeed to share. This 20-page document proved to be a timely gift for his children, for he was killed in a plane crash before the year was out. But he left a legacy richer than stocks and bonds.

I don't think the philosopher Montaigne was altogether correct when he said that although we may be learned with the learning of others, we can be wise only with our own wisdom. There is undoubtedly a difference in the way that wisdom is absorbed and accepted, the way it is exercised and vindicated. I can accept some mathematical and scientific fact as being factual, for example, but it won't necessarily make any difference in the quality of my way of life, even though I have no doubt about it and have ways of verifying its actuality.

Although wisdom has to pass through the head in some way, it has more to do with the heart. That's why philosopher William James was right on the mark when he wrote: "If your heart does not want a world of moral reality, your head will assuredly never make you believe in one."

But people in general are open to the claims of wisdom, which has to do with true morality, which is the art of being human. It is my experience that even the most cynical and turned-off students are honestly hungry for some honest information on how truly to be happy at being human. In such cases, there is even a special wisdom about how to communicate wisdom—"men must be taught as though you taught them not."

Teachers and people in a teaching position have a special advantage on this score. In his excellent book, *The Art of Teaching*, Gilbert Highet makes a point that needs remembering: "Many teachers tend to forget how valuable the wide reading and accumulated experience of a mature man or woman can be to a pupil who is still groping around helplessly among untried experiments and unread books. If you can send him into the world with frames of reference suggested by you, and tricks of craftsmanship which he could get only from you, you will have made him your pupil as much as he ever will be, and earned a right to his permanent gratitude."

Earlier this year I had the chance to give a series of talks to a group of young people who were in an especially difficult and depressing situation. I had often read articles about "my favorite books," or "the 10 books I would like to take with me if I were going to be marooned on a desert island."

So, for this particular series of talks, I thought I would look back over my life and ask myself what were the 10 or so most helpful and illuminating insights I had gained from the wisdom of others, as well as from my own experiences and mistakes. ("Wisdom," said Bernard Baruch, "keeps you from making mistakes, and comes from having made plenty of them.")

No doubt, what each man learns about life, especially about solving its problems or living with its insoluble ones, is often a matter of unlearning earlier ideas or emotional prejudices. So there is bound to be a uniquely personal element in any man's list of his most prized convictions.

But I hold the belief that people are more alike than they are unlike, particularly when there is a question of basic human wants and frustrations. So a man can not only learn from others, but he can pass on to others much that he has learned. The rest of the chapters in this book are based on the talks I gave to a group of young men who needed help in solving soluble problems and in surviving creatively with insoluble ones. And that's a task which faces every man and woman, especially in the pressure chamber known as contemporary civilization.

My list of "favorite insights" will include elements such as the value of emotions, the role of honest humility, the cultivation of a sense of wonder, the necessity of delight, the art of self-knowledge, the primacy of love, a philosophy of frustration, and cop-

22

ing with the terrible hours.

If this list prompts a reader to make his own insights more conscious and to compare his own experiences with those of another, it will serve a useful function. Life, in any case, teaches a man to be modest about the ideas which seem most certain and most important to him at any given moment. There is a story about a young psychologist who at first gave a talk entitled, "Ten Commandments for Raising Your Children." Then he had a few children of his own. So he altered his topic to "Five Rules for Raising Your Children." As his own youngsters advanced through their teens, his topic became: "A Few Suggestions for Raising Your Children."

I would like to end these introductory remarks by making a key affirmation, one which strikes me as urgently needed in these highly pressurized times. It is this: It is all right to be human. It is all right to have feelings and to have human limitations. It is all right to be who you are, and to be able to do only what you reasonably can do in those increasing circumstances where you can't do very much at all. It is all right to have negative feelings—to be angry, confused, frustrated, fed up and let down—whether these feelings are directed toward God, the Church, or life in general.

Don't say: I know I shouldn't feel this way. *Shouldn't* has got nothing to do with feeling. Feelings are automatic responses to some kind of signal in our mind and/or body. Only if we allow ourselves to acknowledge the fact of certain feelings, only if we allow our feelings the right to exist—only then can we reasonably set about finding the true meaning of the signals and deciding the most creative way of responding to the feelings. All the witnesses should have their say before the judge renders a verdict.

23

In his most recent work, *The Angry Book*, Dr. Theodore Rubin makes some telling observations about this whole business of feelings: "I believe you either feel all your feelings or eventually none at all. You cannot select which feelings you will feel and which you won't. . . . Negate anger, and you also negate love."

Anger and frustration are bound to be on the increase during the kind of upheaval civilization is now going through. Even the people who are not feeling so very angry and frustrated are going to have to deal with people who are increasingly feeling that way. So there is much to be gained by a deeper understanding of how feelings in general work, and especially these "less respectable" feelings.

Rollo May, in his *Love and Will*, points out an encouraging phenomenon: "A thing which never fails to surprise a person in therapy is that after he has admitted his anger, animosity and even hatred for a spouse, he ends with feelings of love toward his partner. A patient finds that he represses his love while he suppresses his aggression. Hate and love are not polar opposites; they go together, particularly in transitional ages like ours."

The point I would like to stress is that there is always the possibility of a *human* response to any situation, and ultimately the truly human response is the most satisfactory and healing one. And a human response must be to a great extent a response of feeling, human feeling.

Whether we like it or not, the 70's are probably going to be an extension and an expansion of the shaken 60's. As earthlings, as Americans, as Christians, we are going to have feelings, many and strong,

24

about the developments ahead. So we might as well have wholesome and confident feelings about our feelings. To this topic at some length the next chapter will be devoted. ●

A man with powerful emotions may have more than his share of pain and problems . . . but the emotions with which he is endowed are full of promise, waiting to become the bridge to deep human satisfaction.

Our human choice is not between pain and no pain, but between the pain of loving and the pain of not loving.

2

Terrible Tigers and

Gorgeous Orchids

A S A YOUNGSTER of four or five, my sister was once asked at dinner what part of the chicken she would like. She pondered for a few seconds, and then answered very seriously: "The body."

A body is what we get as part of our human heritage. Our body is so much a part of us that even those modern philosophies which do not deny the spiritual element in man are tending to say that man "is" a body, rather than that he "has" a body.

In any case, because we are bodily creatures we are creatures of emotion, of feeling, affectivity, mood and sensuality. Here I want to use such words in contrast to pure, cold logic and reason, and to sheer will power.

An instant warning is called for. Although we can think of man's animal qualities as distinct from his rational qualities, in his actual functioning man is a single unit simultaneously manifesting rational as well as animal qualities—and here I intend no degrading implications about the idea of animality. On this earth, human behavior is never purely rational or purely emotional. There are only variations in the way that the two ingredients are combined.

One of my "most valued insights" concerns the power and the importance of the emotions. I now believe that the only cure for bad feelings is good feelings, that only creative feelings can outwit destructive feelings. I believe that our "wild and animalistic" times are not suffering from too much feeling but from too little. In fact, my vote would be that the curse of our age is a certain feelinglessness, a fear of deep, genuine and ample emotion. In some extreme cases, G. K. Chesterton's words are verified—"a lunatic is someone who has lost everything except his reason."

What I would like to stress is the fierce reality of emotionality, the immensity of it, the preciousness of it, the inescapability of it, the perils of trying to deny it, the temptations we have to deny it, and the supreme importance of dealing creatively with this endowment of our nature—an endowment which is, at various times, simple and complicated, messy and purifying, painful and sublime. Emotions are a prime source of pressure and a potential remedy for too much pressure.

Stated as an argument, my chief point would be this: A man becomes fully human and humane, becomes what God means him to be, becomes healingly meaningful to others, sees what there is to see about any important human issue, and achieves interior strength and peace to the extent that he recognizes his emotionality, accepts it, frees its potential, and integrates it into his whole self and his whole way of living.

Put in a negative way, my argument would be: To

28

the degree that a man consciously or unconsciously resents and rejects his emotionality, he will be alienated from himself and from others. He will impoverish his own existence and cut himself off from deep bonds with other people. As a religious person he will be in danger of becoming what Gerald Vann called "an immaculate misconception"—correct, pure and proper, perhaps; but not warm and winning, touching and in touch.

One of my college textbooks contained a remark which keeps coming back to mind with growing persuasiveness. "Reason," it said, "is but a speck on the sea of emotion." That speck, like the relatively small rudder of a ship, is undeniably precious—immeasurably so. But without the wind upon the sea, without the force of the waves, the buoyancy of the water, the simultaneous resistance and cooperation of the sea and its ever-present supportive underpinning, the ship will make no progress.

Or, to change the image: Man's rationality is like a paralyzed wheelchair patient who is dependent upon a blind nurse. The patient can see where he wants to go or where he should go. But he needs the energy of the unseeing nurse if he is to get there. Happy the patient who gets along well with his nurse.

This patient-nurse comparison, however, can be misleading. There is a sense in which our feelings can sometimes see more clearly than our minds, in which our senses can be more sensible than our brains. In describing "the fully functioning person," Carl Rogers writes: "Man's behavior is exquisitely rational, moving with subtle and ordered complexity toward the goals his organism is endeavoring to achieve. The tragedy for most of us is that our defenses keep us from being aware of this rationality, so that consciously we are moving in one direction, while organismically we are

29

moving in another."

As the word "emotion" reveals, emotion is the source of motion, of energy, of force, of movement, of propulsion. Here are God-given reservoirs of priceless fuel, waiting to be discovered and tapped and channeled. Such is also true, perhaps especially true, of what is called our "unconscious." Here lie invaluable pay dirt and rich undersoil. True, this subzone is like a jungle. Raw, savage energies are there—blind willfulness, infantile rages, barbarous cravings and lusts and hostilities. Terrible tigers lurk there, but gorgeous orchids grow there too.

Just as the most gracious and heavenward tree is the one which has sunk its roots most deeply into the tenacious soil, so can our most worthy aspirations draw energy and support from this richly endowed underworld. Happy the man who feels that this mysterious part of his nature is fundamentally good and redeemable, and who learns how to master it.

Two other images from the animal world suggest themselves here. A frisky horse can certainly be more trouble than a sleepy one which drags the ice-cart down the back alley. But if you wanted to win a race, you know which horse you would prefer.

Similarly, a man with powerful emotions may have more than his share of pain and problems, and at times he may envy the more apathetic man. But the emotions with which he is endowed are full of promise, waiting to become the bridge to deep human satisfaction. Psychologist Rollo May has pointed out that even neurotic pain is a heartening sign that energy is available for needed changes and better enjoyment of life.

For the second image, think of a powerful, undomesticated dog which a man might inherit. If he is afraid of it, he can put it in his basement and lock the door, throwing it pieces of raw meat from time to time. But he will never really be comfortable with it in his own house, and would be terrified of going down into the cellar where the lonely dog grows more savage.

Or, he can introduce the dog into his companionship, discipline it, occasionally wrestle with it, be growled at and snapped at by it. But eventually and hopefully the animal will become domesticated and humanized, turning into a pleasurable companion. This analogy can be easily applied to human nature and its animal energies, especially that of sexuality.

Sexuality is a force which is so thoroughly suffused through one's entire human identity that a person is really asking for trouble if he tries to suppress it fearfully into his basement, instead of allowing it to unfold naturally within his whole personality. This unfolding will normally require, from time to time, a conscious, head-on slapping down of raw, unintegrated and depersonalized manifestations.

But this deliberate disciplining aims not to destroy sexual sensitivity or to banish it into the outer darkness, but to domesticate and humanize it. Sexual energy is so much a part of us that it cannot be successfully banished anyway. It will only go underground and fester in the clammy dark. Here it will only grow more ferocious, vexatious and threatening, and will eventually insist on surfacing in various disguises and wreak its vengeance in manifold masked ways.

Here it may be timely to recall the correct notion of chastity, meekness and other "bodily" virtues as interior transformations of bodily energies themselves, rather than as cold and rigid clamps superimposed from without—clamps which leave the energies themselves fundamentally unchanged, eager to

31

erupt into rawness if the restraints are removed. Similarly, the horse or dog becomes well trained when the discipline instilled by the master becomes interiorized within the animal itself. The animal now reacts spontaneously in a domesticated way, as by a second nature.

On this point, C. S. Lewis coined one of his many memorable phrases when he said that the brain must fight the belly with the chest. By the brain he meant the pitiably weak force of sheer reason or will power, as contrasted with the belly—crude, self-centered and untamed animal impulses. The chest is an intermediate zone where hearty bodily energies are structured into patterns of reasonableness.

In this zone a man develops qualities like enthusiasm, courage, aggressiveness, endurance of pain, and life-loving self-control. Here he furnishes himself with a cushion, a shock absorber for the brittle bones of rationality. Here he nurtures qualities of moral good taste and achieves that ideal of education which John Ruskin conceived to be not merely the knowledge of what is good and evil, but the visceral love of what is good and loathing of what is evil.

If the arguments made so far are essentially valid, you can easily see why there is something inescapable about man's emotionality, an emotionality based on the very kind of creature he is. If he is alienated from this dimension of his nature, he will be a stranger to himself. Chesterton was right to say, "We do not want joy and anger to neutralize each other and produce a surly contentment. We want a fiercer delight and a fiercer discontent."

On such an understanding of human nature was based St. Augustine's arresting statement that only the passionate heart is pure. Many a man who has fallen into a closed-circuit habit of sexual indulgence can testify what happened when the delight of being loved by another human being entered his life. It might have been expected that erotic involvement would only intensify his sexual sensitivity and aggravate his self-indulgence. Yet many a man has found that a newly discovered personal love, and his felt desire to be worthy of it, actually lessened or entirely eliminated his narcissistic need to fill up an inner vacuum with a basically unsatisfying satisfaction.

Why would a human being strive to suppress his emotionality? The reasons are numerous and a combination of them can be at work in individual cases. A child who is exposed to unhealthily emotional adults may overreact by trying to become rigidly "unemotional." Such an adult could be a parent who was excessively alcoholic, tearful, sentimental, moody, panicky, irascible or argumentative, or an older person who molested or frightened the child in a sexual way.

Or, in responding to gigantic problems which he cannot understand or with which he cannot cope, a child may become terrified by his own overwhelming feelings of hostility, guilt or sensuality. Better no deep feelings at all, he may decide, than any triggering of dangerous feelings like these.

As a person grows he may develop the need to be neat and perfect, but he finds that feelings are untidy. (I know a philosophy teacher who keeps insisting, "If it's human, it's messy.") He may try to protect himself from pain, but finds that emotions make him vulnerable—he prefers an "unconquerable soul." It's as though his accumulation of too well remembered and unabsorbed pain has produced an ingrown toenail in his feelings, so he mustn't let anyone get close enough to step on him.

His insecurity makes him feel he must always be in control, must always see the long road ahead of him, whereas his emotions threaten to heat up his "cool" and muddy up his long-range vision. He doesn't trust the waters of emotion, and doesn't believe he can float on them, so he must be forever swimming. He must anxiously avoid letting the waves of emotion splash dangerously over him and weigh him down like a drowning companion.

For such and similar reasons, a person may also try to reject such wholesome aspects of his personality as tenderness, receptivity, passivity, leisureliness and those exercises of intuition which require silence, stillness, openness, and creative inactivity. He finds it difficult to say with Mary, the Mother of Christ: "Let it be, let it be done, let it be done to me." He must be always the doer, the giver, the changer, the rearranger, the manipulator, the decider, the corrector. It is hard for him to receive a gift, including the gift of existence and the gift of grace, for that would make him dependent on and subject to realities outside himself.

These temptations against emotionality have one common seduction: They promise to save a man from pain. No doubt there are times when a man needs to take it easy, take a break, get away from it all, and give his emotional batteries a chance to recharge and his bruised feelings a chance to heal. By the same token there are times when you are humanly entitled not to answer the doorbell or the telephone.

But the man who tries to achieve a permanent peace by cutting his emotional wires is retreating into a fortress which can become a tomb. This kind of isolation chamber will produce its own kind of pain. Moreover, a man may so wall himself in, so cut himself off, that he may find it impossible to escape or to send out distress signals even if he wants to.

Our human choice, then, is not between pain and

no pain, but between the pain of loving and the pain of not loving. Ask anyone who has tried both ways: No pain is so painful as the pain of isolation, or pain borne in isolation—especially in spiritual isolation from the common brotherhood of human feelings consented to and accepted.

At this point I would like to say a few special things about one particular emotion which gives many people more trouble than they realize, especially people who are trying to take their Christianity seriously, who deeply want to love other people, and who feel obligated to give good example and avoid scandal, who put themselves at the beck and call of other people as they try to be "a man for others." That emotion is wrath and its associated feelings of hostility and aggression. If not rightly handled, this emotion often cloaks itself as depression and fatigue. When not properly recognized it may strike out at such substitute targets as "the red menace," "the establishment" or "the younger generation."

When a speck hits the eye, the eye will automatically blink. When a man is truly frustrated, he will automatically generate a surge of anger. This surge provides him with precious energy, energy to put up a fight, to mobilize and consolidate his inner forces, to knit him protectively together, to brace him for counterattack, and to make him properly reckless at the proper moment.

The power of wrath is a supremely valuable and necessary weapon in the arsenal of any person who takes good and evil seriously and who wants to make an impact on a resisting world. A mature man has learned to express anger at the appropriate targets for the appropriate reason and to an appropriate degree.

Thus the truly meek man does not suppress his anger, but is an expert in applying the energies of wrath. These energies are not frozen but available, and the meek man knows how and when to use them. A man who felt no anger in certain outrageous situations would be failing in virtue, which is another way of saying that at times a man has the duty to be wrathful and to manifest that wrath externally.

Here we may profitably recall a statement of Thomas Aquinas: "Since human nature is made up of body and soul, of an intellectual and a sensitive part, human good demands that a man should surrender himself in his totality to virtue: that is to say, in both his intellectual and sensitive part, and with his body. Hence for human virtue it is necessary that the desire for just vengeance should reside not only in the rational part of the soul but also in the sensitive part and that the body should be moved to serve virtue" (*De Malo,* 12:1).

Elsewhere, and for similar reasons, Aquinas points out that to act *from* passion lessens both praise and blame, while to act *with* passion increases both—because in the latter case a person shows how deeply he is committed by his whole nature to a real or seeming value.

Now if for any reason a person has become afraid of his power of wrath or feels guilty about exercising it, he will find himself in trouble. He may have come to feel afraid or guilty because, for example, as a child those on whom he depended gave him to understand that good children do not have tempers or angry feelings, and that he had better be good if he did not want to be cut off from those on whom he desperately depended.

In any case, there are those who day after day spend tons of energy suppressing their feelings of hostility. This suppression only makes the feelings seem more gigantic and overwhelming. Being unspent on its proper object, the rage may spread out and take on all humanity, the universe and God himself as its eventual target.

A tree grows up, yes, but not to the sky. Anger wants to lash out, but normally it lashes out only to a degree, and then there comes a rebound and relaxation. Our troubled man doesn't realize this emotionally. He doesn't understand William Blake's poem: "I was angry with my friend: I told my wrath, my wrath did end." He does understand the next lines, though: "I was angry with my foe: I told it not, my wrath did grow."

Such repressed wrath can grow to the point of seeming almost infinite, hence most dangerous, hence to express even a little would seem like pulling one's finger out of the dike. Two colossal fears may unconsciously result from this suppression: 1) that this wrath, if expressed, would destroy its object; or else 2) the counterattack would destroy the person showing the anger. It is not necessarily physical death which the frustratedly angry person might dread. He may have a deeper horror of a kind of psychological death in which he would be punished by being cut off by the people he needs. Pent-up anger has this curious way of spreading out infinitely in the imagination, so that a man struggling to bottle up his rage may come to feel that all of humanity and God himself would punish him for lashing out the way he wants to.

Incidentally, a man with great quantities of unspent rage is liable to suppose that other people are as close to a devastating explosion as he is. This supposition may make him extremely uncomfortable in any situation where there is conflict and a show of anger, no matter how legitimate and moderate. It is even conceivable that a pacifist has needed to become so because of an extraordinary amount of unrecognized

37

hostility in his own makeup.

In conclusion, I would like to stress again the need for a man to consent, deep down in his being, to the fact of his emotionality. This I see as a profound act of humility, by which a man affirms his willingness to be what he actually is.

A sign of this willingness is the ability to label feelings by their proper names. A man should not feel guilty about the fact that he has this or that feeling, no matter how selfish or animalistic it may be in itself. Human beings have all sorts of feelings, and it is all right to be human. A man will best be able to manage his feelings creatively and healthily after he has faced and accepted the fact that he has an animal nature and that this animality is essentially good.

A man needs to become convinced that in his emotional makeup, in the very equipment he has, there is a proper combination of emotional possibilities to give him balance and harmony, a harmony produced by the fact that one kind of emotion serves to keep another kind in due proportion—provided all the emotions are in working order. We all come equipped with the proper amount of water wings to keep us emotionally afloat. If we are sinking or lopsided, we just haven't inflated all our equipment.

You don't have to tell a piece of wood how to float. If you free it from a rock holding it down, it will rise to the surface of any body of water. Our natures want to surface healthily, and they will do so automatically if we remove the hindrances.

I am not proposing emotion for emotion's sake, nor am I recommending sentimentality, which is unearned emotion—emotion focused on itself instead of the proper objects of emotion. But our emotionality is a precious bridge to vital aspects of reality, that reality which is our best friend and richest nourishment.

Our mind mustn't lock itself up inside our body and create a demilitarized zone, a no-man's-land where we superficially brush against the outside world and other people. Thinking about these ideas, and vindicating them by experience, we may come to find a new meaning in the fact that one of the most sacred and healing moments of our religion comes when we remember Our Lord's words: "This is my body."

One of the most rewarding by-products of a wholesome and relaxed emotionality is a continuous growth in self-knowledge. The vital art of self-knowledge will be the topic of the next chapter. ●

One of the key quests of a person's life is finding out who he is. Many pressures result when a person doesn't know who he is, or when he tries to become an impossible person.

3

Exploring Inner Space

ALL THE WAY HOME, a movie produced a few years ago, was based on James Agee's Pulitzer Prize-winning novel, *A Death in the Family*. Introducing the novel is a short prologue entitled: "Knoxville: Summer 1915." (American composer Samuel Barber has written a haunting oratorio for parts of the prologue.)

After opening this section with the words: "We are talking now of summer evenings in Knoxville, Tennessee, in the time that I lived there successfully disguised to myself as a child," Agee ends with this poignant reminiscence about his family:

"After a little while I am taken in and put to bed. Sleep, soft, smiling, draws me unto her; and those receive me, who quietly treat me as one familiar and well-beloved in that home, but will not, oh, will not, not ever; but will not ever tell me who I am."

One of the key quests of a man's life is unquestionably finding out who he is. Often enough the members of one's immediate family seem to be the least helpful in that search.

But, in any case, the search is crucial. Many excessive pressures result when a person doesn't know who he is, or when he tries to become an impossible person. A philosophy student of mine once remarked that, as he saw it, most people are on a journey from what they are not to what they cannot be. For his part, poet e. e. cummings warned that the world is a giant conspiracy to make everybody over into somebody else.

Some of the "most treasured" lessons life has managed to teach me concern this matter of self-knowledge. The lessons assert specifically: Such knowledge is 1) necessary
 2) difficult
 3) possible and
 4) worthwhile.

The pursuit of self-knowledge might be topically described as the exploration of inner space. In its own way such exploration can require more skill and courage than exploring outer space. As poet W. B. Yeats put it (before the moon age): "Why should we honour those that die upon the fields of battle; a man may show as reckless a courage in entering into the abyss of himself."

I'd like to begin this reflection on self-knowledge with a parable. Picture a little boy alone on a wide beach. Before him stretches the unbounded ocean. Behind him rear high cliffs which he cannot climb. How he got there he doesn't know, but for the moment he is enjoying himself as he plays in the sand.

Suddenly the sky grows dark, the air turns chilly and the tide starts coming in. From lack of experience there are two precious items of information which es-

42

cape the child: 1) The tide comes in, but it also goes out; 2) you don't have to drown in water; you can swim or float if you know how.

Not knowing these facts, the boy becomes panicky. He notices a wooden crate nearby, runs to it, pulls it over to the cliff, scrambles up on it, and sits there huddling and shivering with his eyes closed. Perhaps he even passes out momentarily from fear.

In any event, when he opens his eyes again, he finds that the tide has receded. He has been saved. And no doubt the wooden crate has been his savior.

So wherever he goes thereafter the crate must go with him. Whether or not he goes to certain places depends on whether or not he can lug his crate along, whether or not there is room for it and no danger that the crate may be lost, damaged or stolen.

And he needs the crate often, not merely when he is near the ocean. For even the sound of running water may trigger his nervous memory. Then he must stop whatever he is doing, climb up on the crate and crouch there until he feels safe again.

How does this parable apply? The youngster might have been any one of us when we underwent some severe emotional threat in our childhood, a threat which came from outside ourselves or from some inner experience. Feeling trapped and in peril, not grasping the nature of our fears, not realizing that emotional tides go out as well as come in and that they can be floated upon, we would have spontaneously sought for some way to protect ourselves. We would have reached out for some crate, some emotional crutch which promised to save us.

Perhaps in its own way this crutch did offer some temporary support. But we may have learned too well to depend on it, and insist on lugging it around as part of our emotional baggage. Like a security blanket, our crate must always be available and safeguarded. When pressure is on, we instantly go into our self-protective routine. This pressure need not be real, however. It is enough if any situation reminds us of our earlier terrifying encounter with the sea.

It isn't too hard to run up against other people's crates. We can detect them in the person who, without any reasonable explanation—even to himself—suddenly gets angry or moody, or silent or nervous; the person who shows strange inconsistencies, is dependably unreliable, who seems incapable of being serious, or of being relaxed, or of taking a stand, or of being attentive, or of admitting ignorance, or of accepting a gift, or of saying no.

What we may be witnessing in these situations is some kind of compulsion, some automatic response which, for the moment at least, is not able not to occur.

What we may need to do if we are going to grow and to continue to grow is to become aware of the crates we may be carrying around within ourselves, find out gradually why we load ourselves down with them, where we acquired them and, eventually, how to get rid of them. If we are lucky, some decisive experience may help us to short-circuit this whole conscious route, and inaugurate a healthier, more rewarding pattern of response which will cause the earlier pattern to wither away.

A neurosis may be defined as a bad case of crates. Or, more precisely, a neurosis may result from the fact that we simultaneously want our crates and don't want them. We sense their disadvantages, but are not ready to give up their advantages.

The point about a neurosis is that it *is* a solution to a problem, only it is an inadequate solution, or a bad solution, or an outgrown solution. Because we feel that we need our crates, and need them badly, we will hold on desperately to them, disguising them if necessary, and fiercely resisting anyone who tries to tamper with them or dismantle them.

This is one reason why psychotherapy is so often time consuming, threatening and painful. What the therapist is often trying to do is to get close enough to the patient to uncover with him his secret crates, motivate him to dismantle them, and prepare him for the moment when the tide comes in, the crate is useless, and the patient must face the water cratelessly and prove to himself in a *felt* way (and not just an intellectual way) that the tide also goes out, and that he can float in the meantime, and even do a bit of swimming.

As a healing art, psychiatry is relatively young and is undergoing much development and criticism from within and without. But perhaps a word can be said here about the ideal relationship between doctor and patient, as envisaged by many therapists. Each person is like a switchboard operator manipulating the machinery of his emotions. If the equipment is being incorrectly used, a technician is needed—not to tell the operator which calls to place, but how to use the machinery if any calls are to be placed at all.

Ideally, then, a therapist does not tell a patient which values to choose, or which specific goals to aim for in his life. Rather he aims to liberate within the patient enough emotional freedom to enable him to choose humanly.

The point is worth mentioning here, since many of us are called upon to "counsel" one another in our daily lives. As good listeners, we can often make our best contributions by letting another person sort out his feelings in our presence, let him see what contradictions may be at work, and encourage him to

45

exercise the responsibility of freedom.

A few other points about our emotions merit mentioning.

First, our feelings have superb memories. Hence, in many situations we are not so much responding to a present reality as to a remembered reality—an incident of the past of which we have been reminded. With that reminder old feelings are stirred anew, feelings which may not be appropriate to the situation actually confronting us. To the degree that we have the emotional freedom to respond to the true situation which is making a fresh demand on us, we have the power of response ability.

Secondly, we sometimes speak of feelings as "irrational," "unreasonable," "erratic," and "inconsistent." Yet, given our personal history and experience, there is a strong inner logic to the ways we respond. If the "major premise" or underlying supposition of the emotional syllogism were clearly spelled out, we would see how logical the rest of the syllogism is. The trouble is that we often operate under the influence of unexpressed presumptions, premises which may indeed lie hidden even from ourselves.

A third point: Every neurosis, every pattern of compulsive and unfree emotional response, can be seen as an exaggerated virtue. In other words, the problem may not be the *kind* of response we are making, but the intensity and inflexibility of it.

Cleanliness, politeness, self-reliance, standing up for principle, discipline—all these are virtuous qualities. But when these qualities take on a grim, restless, unyielding aspect, when they operate to the detriment of other qualities, then the neurotic element is revealing itself not in the virtue but in the exaggeration, the lack of balance, the inhuman rigidity.

There is a plus and a minus side to this aspect of

unfree behavior. The minus sign, in terms of self-knowledge, is that the "virtuous" aspect of our neurotic tendencies can blind us to the exaggerated aspect. But there is reassurance in the possibility that we may already have enough of a needed quality and our chore is chiefly to temper the element of exaggeration.

On this score a favorite story of mine tells of a lady who told a psychiatrist that her family thought she ought to see a doctor because she liked pancakes. "Why," the doctor replied, "there is nothing abnormal about liking pancakes. I'm rather fond of them myself." "You are!" answered the lady delightedly. "You must come to my house sometime. I have six trunks full in the attic."

So much for these preliminary remarks about the difficulty of self-knowledge. I want to talk awhile about the necessity of such knowledge.

There is a saying which for me contains the key to this necessity: "The roots of the eyes are in the heart." In other words, what we see of reality, the evidence which we uncover and the relative value we accord to various probabilities, depend not just on our physical eyes and our brainpower. What we see depends at times on what we are, on our "heart condition." There are essential moments when our vision is a revelation of ourselves, our deep, inner, truest self.

So it is that when I affirm that two plus two is four, I may have spoken the truth, but it is not a vital *human* truth, and it hasn't told you anything about myself. But if I declare that a man should keep his word, or that "hell is other people," or that nobody is to be trusted, or that "the worst sin is to make what is concrete into something abstract," then I am telling you something about myself, and I am telling you (rightly or wrongly) about the true way to live as a human being.

In this respect, the total self is like a lens through which we probe human truths. When the stars in this heaven seem blurred or faded out, the trouble may be in the telescope rather than in the stars. In the science of human truths, our whole selves are a key part of the research equipment. One of our prime tasks as men is to purify, polish and focus rightly the lens of our own selfhood.

We can profitably recall here the words of Jesus to some of his ill-disposed listeners: "You do not come to the light because you hate the light and rather love the darkness." A man whose face is blemished might prefer to keep that face hidden from the light, so that neither he nor others can see the true picture—even though the light may be the best medicine for healing what is hurting.

In this kind of situation we have an explanation for what is an undeniable fact: that there are times when everybody else can plainly see what a man cannot or will not see about himself. Everybody knows that a certain man is becoming an alcoholic, or is ruining his marriage and hurting his children by too much work, or is pursuing a woman for romantic reasons. Yet he does not see what is plain to others because—the roots of the eyes are in the heart.

Now, there are areas of life—important areas— where this truth is not necessarily very important. Such would be the scientific area. All sorts of "objective" data exist which are clearly there for everyone to see.

But this fact is of immeasurable value when it comes to deciding basic human issues such as the existence of God, the meaning of life and of virtues like truthfulness, honesty and integrity. Here everything may turn upon the influence of a man's unconscious desires, hates, fears and needs.

For this reason it seems to me absolutely essential that when a man wants to make fundamental decisions about his life as a whole and to see human issues in all their fullness, he must try to bring *all* of himself to bear upon *all* of the question. For a man himself is a part, and a decisive part, of what he sees in such matters.

Self-knowledge, then, is an admittedly difficult, but a most necessary art. It is an art which seems to have very little to do with intelligence and other talents as such. In point of fact, the brainier a person is, the more ingenious he may be at masking himself from himself, and making excuses for himself.

On the other hand, the world has a large supply of simple, unsophisticated and not noticeably intellectual people who have remarkable gifts of insight about themselves and other people. It's as though a deep love for honesty has strengthened their human vision and given them a taste for the difference between what is sham and what is authentic. Others might spend a whole lifetime denying the obviousness of a truth which these souls can see in a second.

Seeing the truth about one's destiny in life is very much a matter of listening attentively and unfearfully to the deepest wishes of your own heart. How often people, especially young people, think they want something themselves when they really want what somebody else wants for them. Or else they reject something because somebody else wants it for them.

In neither case do they take their own wishes seriously. Here I am not referring to passing whims, but to inclinations born out of the deepest and most prized convictions and experiences of a life. Theologically, there is much to be said for the idea that "inclination" is a sign of "vocation." Yet the inclination has to be our own, not that of our parents.

The opposite is true too. Yet many young people, going through a rebellious stage, reject a value just because a parent affirms it. These youths fail to see that by so acting they are actually placing their parent in a controlling position. If the parent says "no," they feel compelled to say "yes." Hence the parent is still calling the shots, and the youngster is still tied to the parent, though in a negative way. Fortunately, many young people come to see that they can't be free until they make their own choice, regardless of the pressure (positive or negative) of a parent or any other human nonself.

The person who allows his peer group to dictate his wishes is similarly an unfree person. So you find that many a youngster, having smashed all the things his peers decide ought to be smashed, having allowed them to dictate what he ought to be against, ends up not knowing what he is for. He hasn't yet really taken his own inclinations seriously enough.

A former seminarian of my acquaintance once wrote: "For some reason, I don't know why, the apostolic life always held a terror for me. Even in the minor seminary I tried to shake the terror off or quit. But my confessor would say, 'When you're lying on your deathbed, son, think to yourself, would you rather die having led a priestly life or a lay one?' Now there's a dilemma to put to a young idealist. So I kept that vision before me into the major seminary.

"On the side I studied up on the theology of a vocation. To my surprise I found that if you don't like the life of a priest, you don't have a vocation. Where had that simple idea been for eight years?"

No doubt in this time of major change within the Church, many people in religious life are feeling the loss of accidental securities which prevented them from acknowledging their own innermost feelings about the life they once chose. What they do next is another question, one which can be very complicated. Yet surely there are some who are finding their vocation when they seem to be losing it.

Such dilemmas might never had occurred if such persons had been embodying the wisdom of Carl Roger's description of the "fully functioning person: He is making use of all his organic equipment to sense, as accurately as possible, the existential situation within and without. He is using all the data his nervous system can thus supply, using it in awareness, but recognizing that this total organism may be, and often is, wiser than his awareness."

Striving for such wisdom is a sacred thing, especially if inclination is truly a sign of vocation. Here, then, is a fundamental reason why self-knowledge is necessary. In the next chapter some thought will be given to possible means for mastering the art, and some additional reasons why that art is worthwhile cultivating. ●

Jesus said: "The truth will make you free." How fortunate we are when we learn that truth is good for us, that we are made for it, and that it is our friend . . . what a blessing to discover that you don't have to be as clever, intelligent, successful, popular, athletic or famous as you thought you had to be!

4

Polishing the Lens
of Selfhood

HOW TO LIVE CREATIVELY and humanly in the midst of pressure, especially the super-pressures of our dizzying age. That is the question on which this book is trying to throw some tested light.

So far, I've stressed the crucial role of emotions and feelings, and the difficult but necessary art of self-knowledge. Such knowledge is possible and it is eminently worthwhile, as I hope to show in the following paragraphs.

In his first volume of poetry, published more than half a century ago, Robert Frost included a 12-line poem called *Revelation*. He ends by saying:

> But so with all, from babes that play
>   At hide-and-seek to God afar,
> So all who hide too well away
>   Must speak and tell us where they are.

We ourselves are among those "who hide too well away" from ourselves. Hence the need for pursuing self-knowledge. Actually, this is a lifelong quest. At the physical level a man may never discover that he has a certain bone or muscle problem until he tries to perform a specific kind of activity.

At the personal level, we find that the changing challenges of life force us into new areas of action and give us an ever-deepening and -expanding insight into ourselves. These insights can be surprising at times. People, for example, who have long thought of themselves as quite liberal, permissive and open-minded when they had no authority, are sometimes amazed to unearth within themselves a strong streak of intolerance or bossiness once they shoulder the power and responsibility of authority.

But, to paraphrase the words of Robert Frost, there are voices which "speak and tell us" where we are, where our feelings and needs and possibilities lie. Here, in my experience, are some of the most helpful sources of revealing voices:

1) Pay attention to the kind of people who make you feel angry, uncomfortable or threatened. Revelation may be waiting here, as suggested by the definition of a "bore" as someone who talks about himself when you want to talk about yourself.

Ask yourself what seems special about such bothersome people. Whom do they perhaps remind you of? What kind of hurt do you think they could inflict on you? Why would they be likely to do so? Do other people seem to react to them differently than you do? What causes the difference?

In such probings there isn't necessarily any question of who is right and who is wrong, but simply of what happens in your feelings and why. Don't mask your feelings by the thought that you shouldn't feel

54

that way. As I mentioned in a previous chapter, *shouldn't* has got nothing to do with feelings as such.

2) Notice the kind of people you admire. Why precisely do you admire them? What do they have that you would like to have? What makes you think you don't already have it? What advantage would result from your being like them? What disadvantages are you suffering because you are not like them?

3) What do you think about when you are not thinking about anything? Daydreams can provide us with precious clues to our inner world and the use we are making of our subterranean energies.

It has been said that a man's character is dyed the color of his leisure thoughts. This may be too strong a way of putting it, since our so-called leisure thoughts may often reflect our inborn temperament and our unconscious world—realities for which we may have little or no responsibility.

Hence it might be better to describe our "character" as what we do with our temperament. But our character can manage our temperament more skillfully and productively if we know our temperament well. And on this score our daydreams and fantasies (and even our night dreams) can help us very much.

4) Give some thought to what people say to you when they are angry. People in anger often want to hurt us, and they may well choose some weak spot, some touchy point at which to aim their fiery arrows. After the wound has healed, we might have something useful to learn by quietly wondering why our adversary elected to say or do what he did rather than something else.

5) Remember the law of opposites. If, on a windy day, you flew over a lake and saw a man leaning heavily to the left side of his sailboat, you could reasonably guess without further information that his

55

sailboat is probably being blown heavily to the right.

In a similar way, the vigilante who is extraordinarily preoccupied with bad movies or bad magazines may be telling you something about his own inner fears and compulsions. Or the exceedingly unpugnacious man may be wrestling inside himself with an explosive amount of pent-up hostility. And the youngster who repeatedly tells you how much he likes his father may be trying to drown out the voice of some contrary feeling within himself.

Freud coined the expression "reaction formation" to describe this kind of "bending over backwards." Such an unconscious tendency is at work, for example, in the mother who overprotects her child as a reaction against some actual feelings of her own which are hostile to the child, but which she cannot allow herself consciously to admit and accept.

In the midst of your next emotional storm, you might profitably test out this notion of opposites. Could there be a masked ball going on, with the Capulets dressed up as Montagues, and vice versa? Could the thing being fought against be really the thing that is being sought? People sometimes rave because they have been fired from a job, when at some level of their feelings, they had really wanted to be fired. And then, of course, there are the people who actually enjoy their ill health, and find in their anxiety and problems a source of some kind of emotional satisfaction.

Whenever you try to achieve emotional insight and honesty, never be satisfied with the first explanation of your feelings which comes to mind. This explanation may be true enough at its own level, but it may not go deep enough to produce the needed light. From the emotional point of view, there is generally an answer behind the answer, and possibly a third answer behind that. (When no puzzling problem or inconsistency exists, there is no need to analyze your every feeling —a practice which in itself may be an excuse for not acting.)

I myself can recall some very hostile feelings aroused by a seminary teacher who didn't give a very good course. I was angry because the course was bad and boring, true. But I finally realized that I was even more angry because the teacher wasn't giving me what I thought I needed. Specifically, I felt I needed "intellectual" answers to certain problems, answers which would take care of all possible adversaries. If I couldn't give these answers (so I imagined) I would feel painfully inadequate, stupid, vulnerable, and a failure.

I came to see that the fear of intellectual failure, of not being able to meet everyone's demand, was my greatest concern and was causing the intense degree of my hostility. As I have long since discovered, "intellectual" answers are not the deepest answers anyway— and most people knew that better than I did at the time. In any case, there was no law forbidding me to search out on my own the kind of answers I was looking for. Of course, that would have required some special energy and initiative on my part.

The art of finding the answer beneath the answer, the feeling behind the feeling, involves a great deal of practice and a willingness to find at work some immature and not very lofty motivations. The philosopher Kierkegaard talked about eavesdropping on the secret murmurings of the heart, which is a good way to put the matter. He also spoke of his desire to catch his thoughts with their umbilical cords still attached— before the mind loses sight of their specialness and their uniqueness, and rudely catalogues them in groups of similar or related thoughts.

In that respect, our minds can behave like a clerk who is sorting out mail in a business office and who just looks at the name, and automatically shoots the letter into a given slot. He doesn't notice the handwriting, the stamp, the postmark, the kind of envelope. Just so the mind that classifies thoughts and feelings too quickly can overlook important clues and meanings.

In the Gospel we see Jesus taking a deaf man aside from the crowd, and putting his finger into his ear. To sharpen our own hearing, we need to pull aside from the noisy crowds and drown out distracting sounds. On this score we are all in need of "hearing aids."

As he pursues the treasure of self-knowledge, blessed is the man who has a genuine friend, a person with whom he can be candid, who accepts him "warts and all," and with whom he can compare notes about what it means to be human in various situations. It's hard to tell if you're marching in step if you look only at your own feet. Neither can you tell if your responses or interpretations are basically human and understandable if you have no way of comparing your inner experience with that of other people.

Not that everyone must march in step in every respect. In the imagery given by Henry David Thoreau, we are entitled to march by the drummer we hear in the depths of our own being. But it is valuable not to be mistaken about the drummers that other people hear. And when it comes to certain basic human values, there is much to be said for the likelihood that we all hear the same drummer.

We may often find that the clue to our response in any situation is not the fact that we had the response, but in the intensity of that response. When Harry Truman was President, a group of men from Puerto Rico kept reading in the newspapers sharp criticisms of the President and of Congress. Many Americans were obviously very angry. So were those Puerto

Ricans. So they tried to assassinate the President, and burst into the Congressional chambers shooting away.

When the expected revolution of Americans did not occur, the would-be assassins were astounded. No doubt, many Americans were angry at their government, but they weren't *that* angry. The gunmen made the mistake of projecting the explosiveness of their private feelings onto others who had similar feelings, but not to any explosive degree.

The rewards for working at self-knowledge are many and eminently worthwhile. As Jesus said, the truth will make you free. How fortunate we are when we learn that the truth is good for us, that we are made for it, and that it is our best friend. As William James pointed out, "To give up pretensions is as blessed a relief as to have them gratified." What a blessing to discover that you don't have to be as clever, intelligent, successful, popular, athletic or famous as you thought you had to be!

Love for the truth, and openness to it, forge the sturdy kind of bond which we all seek to have with others. I know a married couple who are very passionately concerned about the vital human issues and problems of today's world. They often debate vigorously about these points and feel no need to acquiesce limply in the view of the other. Because they both agree on the importance of true answers, they can disagree forcibly about particulars. What unites them is their readiness to shed any pretensions or prejudices, and their belief that each can help the other do that and is loving the other by helping him do that.

Self-knowledge doesn't necessarily and immediately remove all the immature habits of self-defense which we may have built up over a long period. Neither does some genuine insight instantly repair all the damage which we may have done to ourselves at the emotional level. As Cardinal Newman put it, you may burn the stick, but that doesn't heal the wound.

But the situation is like a man who habitually rushed into a dark room and smashed into a heavy desk just inside the door. Finally he gets a better picture of his behavior. He mightn't be able to remove the desk right away, but at least he can school himself to enter more slowly. turn on the lights, and walk around the desk instead of into it.

In this whole matter, it is encouraging to realize that we have an inbuilt gravitation toward balance, health and wholesomeness. Reality is our best friend, not illusion. And we come equipped with powerful radar cuing us into reality.

C. S. Lewis wrote: "What I like about experience is that it is such an honest thing. You may take any number of wrong turnings; but always keep your eyes open and you will not be allowed to go very far before the warning signals appear. You may have deceived yourself, but experience is not trying to deceive you. The universe rings true wherever you fairly test it."

Another advantage of self-knowledge is this: We are more like other people than we are different. Hence he who knows himself better, knows human nature better, and is in a better position to understand and help other people.

At a deeper level, self-knowledge brings with it the possibility of coming to know the Creator better. St. Augustine used to pray: "May I know me, may I know Thee." God alone can satisfy the profoundest hungers in man, and a man who through self-knowledge comes to know these hungers better gains fresh insight into the meaning of God for him.

Self-knowledge will teach a man much about the genuine meaning, power and importance of love. Simultaneously, a man will learn more about that God who

60

is love. My belief is that in the ultimate recesses of the human heart what we want out of love for ourselves is what God wants for us out of his love for us.

I'd like to mention one particular danger about the quest for self-knowledge. Many people, perhaps most, are not sufficiently reflective, and their defenses against wholesome self-discovery are built rather high, wide and deep. But some people are unhealthily introspective—though this trait can be a defense against seeing the obvious or against committing themselves to the kind of action which would produce genuine self-knowledge.

In any case, a person can go after self-knowledge like an ill-inspired biologist who might go cutting into a body with a knife to find out where the "life" is. Or he can burn into his emotional innards like a searing sunbeam shining through a powerful magnifying glass.

I am far from recommending such a brutal, head-on procedure, especially by a person who is motivated by self-hatred or self-pity, or who is already excessively self-centered. (Besides, our defenses are pretty clever, and we often get our best clues indirectly, out of the corner of our eye, and quite gradually.)

I am recommending the productive kind of self-knowledge which an athlete might gain by relaxedly and confidently watching films of himself in action, or which a man might achieve by enjoyably studying his own ancestry and visiting his forebears' homestead.

A number of basic Christian beliefs, if accepted by the heart and not just by the head, should help a man pursue this healthy kind of self-knowledge. There is the conviction that God loves him, that human nature as created by God is fundamentally good, that forgiveness is possible, failings are universal, mistakes are reversible, that humility as a virtue consists of a man's consenting to be what he is and to do what he can.

61

There is the belief, finally, that just as Jesus took on human nature and used it as an instrument of healing and reconciliation, so even with its inborn and accumulated limitations, our human nature can be and is meant to be a source of healing in this world. Limitations are no limitation. By being male, Jesus could not be female; by being a Jew he could not be a Greek; by living in Palestine he couldn't live in Europe; by living when he did, he could not historically do his founding work in some other century. Still, he did what he could within the limitations he faced. The Father blessed that work, as he will ours.

In this whole process of achieving maturity, Lazarus of the Scriptures serves as an excellent model for special reasons. Although Christ raised him from the dead, he was still bound up, face and body. Jesus didn't unbind him, but told others to do so (just as others had bound him in the first place) and then to let him go free.

Through lack of love, including our own lack of proper self-love, we bind each other up. To the degree that God's love is operative in us, we will regard it as our duty and our privilege to help unbind our neighbor, and let him help unbind us.

Pilate said, "I have the power to crucify you, and the power to set you free." We are Pilates to one another, and it is Christ who stands before us in the person of our neighbor. Our summons is to set each other free. And the freer we are the more we can help others to liberate themselves.

This mutual service is the theme of a poem of mine:

SYNCHRONIZING IN SECRET

Do you know the true, truly funny story
about the man who each day blew
the noonday factory whistle
having first namelessly checked

by faceless phone
with the woman at the city hall switchboard
for the presumably more official time
when all the time
the selfsame woman was each day
pacing the city hall clock
with the noonday factory whistle?
Wordlessly at times
you check with me, I know,
for courage and for meaning and for
other timely contradictions against
the ages of an evacuated hour
a lightless minute
a savage second.
Won't you be amused to learn someday
that all the besieged, erratic while
I've been setting my heart
by you?

●

Humility is not only the willingness to be what I am. It is also the willingness to do what I can. It's the work of a lifetime.

We don't solve our problems and then start living. We solve our problems by living. We have to learn to live with mistakes, failures and imperfections.

5

The Worth of
Earthiness

S UPPOSE YOU could give just one sermon in your
whole life. What would you choose to talk about,
to get off your chest before a captive audience of your
fellow human beings? G. K. Chesterton, who had an
extraordinary amount of chest, once asked himself this
question. The topic of his choice was, of all things, the
quality of humility.

That quality is the subject of this chapter. For some
of my most treasured insights (though not necessarily
the most practiced) have to do with the honest meaning of this quality. As I have come to understand what
humility is, I see it as an essential tool for handling
necessary pressures creatively, and for avoiding unnecessary pressures successfully.

Humility is not an easy virtue to understand, perhaps because it is not primarily an intellectual affair.
Could it be that the proud misunderstand it, and the
thoroughly humble are somehow unaware of it? In

any case, many of us tend to see it as a sickening lack of personal presence, a refusal to affirm yourself, an absence of gumption and getup, a draining out of your own selfhood and identity, a constant depreciation and devaluation of your own talents and accomplishments, an unwillingness to have opinions, viewpoints and preferences, a dread of being noticed, a passion for anonymity.

Unfortunately, there are people like that, and some of them probably regard themselves as humble. They often seem depressed and are depressing. As Zorba the Greek stands for verve and vitality, they seem to stand for anti-life. They embody the line from the musical play, *Zorba:* "Life is what you do while you are waiting to die."

Such "humility" is more like a synonym for neurosis and masochism. No wonder healthy people reject this notion of the virtue. The poet Swinburne blamed this kind of humility on the "pale" Jesus, and declared that the world had grown gray with his breath. What a travesty, noted Dorothy Sayers, of the man who went through life like a ball of fire.

Then there is the other phony brand of humility which consists in running yourself down in the expectation that this will force people to compliment you. This is humility with a hook. To see its true colors, try an experiment. The next time someone tells you how imperfectly he has performed, answer with a straight face: "Well, that is certainly true, but you undoubtedly did the best you could."

Since the closest thing to a true diamond is a really clever fake, we can expect to have trouble at times distinguishing the genuine jewel of humility from its fraudulent forms. Perhaps a clue to the distinction lies in this: A truly humble person doesn't think little of himself, rather he thinks of himself little.

There is a related distinction between a selfish person and a self-centered person. A selfish person may take his own superiority coolly for granted, spend his time and energy on self-satisfying projects, and have no compunction about the fact that he couldn't care less about what other people think, feel or need.

By contrast, the self-centered person may indeed care much about other people (perhaps too much so), but he has the habit of referring everything to himself, even if by way of criticizing himself and comparing himself unfavorably with everybody else. He hasn't yet learned the blessed joys of forgetting about his private self and splashing around in the waters of objectivity, i.e., in persons and things outside himself.

These remarks have perhaps prepared us for a better and sharper definition of humility as a virtue. The word itself is suggestively connected with the Latin word "humus," which means "ground" or "earth." Abraham Lincoln's remark is right on target here: "A man's legs ought to be long enough to reach the ground." For a humble man is in touch with the good earth, with his own earthiness. He exemplifies the words of philosopher Martin Heidegger: "Growing means this: to open yourself to the breath of heaven and at the same time to sink roots into the darkness of the earth."

Many years ago I heard a functional definition of humility which sheds more and more light the longer I live. Humility, it said, is the willingness to be what you are and to do what you can. Accordingly, the humble man does not merely *recognize* what he is. In itself such recognition is an act of the intellect. But the humble man does more than that. In the depths of his being, he consents to, affirms, ratifies and says yes to what he is.

It was a wise woman who said that the secret of

life is to accept it. Yet there are many ways of not accepting it. An old definition notes that the difference between a psychotic and a neurotic is this: that the psychotic thinks two and two make five; the neurotic knows that two and two make four, but he is not happy about it.

All right. Humility is the willingness to be what I am. But what am I? In a sense, I spend my whole life discovering who I am. But I find out this much in a hurry: I am a creature. I have limits, edges, borders. I am not unbounded, all-knowing, all-powerful, all-gifted, pleasing to all. I am not self-sufficient. I am not God. These are the facts. The question is: Am I willing to be what I am?

What am I? I am dependent. My very physical conception depended on other beings. My survival over the first few years hinged on the attention, care and know-how of other people. I wear clothing that other people have made. I eat food that other people have planted, harvested, transported and cooked. I use vehicles which others have invented and manufactured. I move over roads which others have paved, following routes which others have charted.

I speak a language which others have coined. I read pages which others have printed, containing ideas which others have minted. I am warmed and cooled by the industry and ingenuity of others. I enjoy rights for which others have fought and died. I am nourished by traditions and wisdoms discovered and preserved by others. If I see farther than my ancestors, it is often because I am standing on their shoulders. I need experts and professionals such as doctors, lawyers, dentists, counselors, firemen and policemen.

The fact of my dependence is overwhelmingly clear. The question is, do I approve of this fact? Granted that I should do for myself what I reasonably can, granted

68

that other people need me too, am I at peace with the fact that I must rely on other human beings, some of whom are not always reliable? Do I perhaps resent asking for help? Do I find it hard to say thank you? to accept a gift?

What else am I? I am a limited, dependent creature in the actual world of my own time in history. It is a world whose laws I did not legislate, whose circumstances I did not personally forge. But these laws and circumstances confront me, challenge me, make demands on me. No doubt I can rage against such a situation. As the poet A. E. Housman wrote: "That two and two are four / and neither five nor three / The heart of man has long been sore / And long 'tis like to be."

But whether I'm sore about it or not, there are such things as the law of cause and effect. If I want the effect, I must posit the cause. If I want the goal, I must accept the means. If I want the fruits of things, I must cultivate the roots of things. I once saw a sign outside a church which put the issue well: "The darkest day in a man's life is when he tries to get something for nothing."

If I want to, I am free to rebel against my physical needs for food, sleep and relaxation. I am free to rebel against my own sexuality and the ways it makes me vulnerable and creates the need for discipline. I can rebel against the laws of growth, the way that things take time.

I can rebel against the fact that there are only 60 seconds in a minute, 60 minutes in an hour, and 24 hours in a day. I can rebel against time by scheduling too much, waiting too long, coming late habitually, and forcing others to wait. In all of these ways I can rebel against the creature of time which I am. But that means that I become split within myself, alienated from my own deepest identity.

What am I? I am also a sinner. As playwright Eugene O'Neill put it, I am born broken and am in need of glue. I deal with other people who are also broken, and I live in a flawed, broken world. There is a sense in which I must be willing to accept this fact too—not in the sense that I conspire lazily with evil and sinfulness, but in the sense that I consent to having been born into a world where sinfulness and imperfection have been allowed to be some of the realities.

Humility is not only the willingness to be what I am. It is also the willingness to do what I can. Once again, it is the work of a lifetime for me to discover what I am able to do, both in a general way and in any given situation. It is also essential to discover what is worth doing. This discovery is crucial because I have only a certain amount of time and energy and ability and opportunity. Sooner or later I have to start renouncing objective possibilities because they are not subjectively feasible for me in my concrete circumstances.

The point also arrives when quantity of action becomes the enemy of quality of action. Humility includes the willingness to be a part of the show, to provide a piece of the action. I must be agreeable to "gathering up the fragments," the partialities which are at our disposal, and to letting others contribute to the final mosaic being designed by Providence.

Willing to do what I can, I must come to learn that I cannot and should not try to do everything for other people. You do no favor for a child if you always carry it. It must learn to do its own walking, even at the expense of some bumps and bruises. There are some people who "enjoy" their troubles and who relish the attention such troubles give them and the excuses

70

afforded thereby. You will sink into a quagmire if you rush in and try to save such people directly from their very willful selves.

Others will unconsciously delight in frustrating your best efforts or in capitalizing upon your weak points—your need to be a savior, for instance—and they will detect and milk your unconscious guilt feelings with remarkable ingenuity.

In this matter of doing what we can, we need to be on our guard against the hypocrisy of working up all sorts of *angst* and pity for situations which are largely out of our control, while neglecting or actually aggravating situations which are at hand. There are classic examples in the man who wrote a book on the proper education of children, while consigning his own to an asylum; or the noble Russian women who shed hearty tears for the poor people depicted in an opera while their own peasant coachmen were freezing to death outside the theater.

The point is not that we should be callous to the dreadful problems in Vietnam, Biafra and the ghettos. By all means, let us do what we reasonably and consciously can, though at times this will be precious little in any direct way. But in the meantime we shouldn't forget that there may be spiritual Vietnams 20 feet from us, ghettos of the spirit around the corner, and emotional Biafras right in our own families. (There is an inverted kind of materialism which is generous only to the physical needs of others.) The world will always have more need of men who are willing to live humbly for a good cause than of men who are interested only in dying heroically for a magnificent and self-glorifying cause.

What are some of the signs that I am trying to do more than I realistically can, or trying to do things which no human being can or should really do for another? Well, I am entitled to my suspicions if I find myself growing cynical, morose, depressed, snappish, highly critical of others, negative toward the efforts of others, corrosively doubtful of the decency, goodwill and basic honesty of large groups of human beings. (The cynic, it has been said, is the man who never smells flowers without looking for the coffin.)

Then it may be time to inquire just how much the situation in question bothers me for objective reasons, and how much it *bothers* me because it bothers *me*, and reminds me of my own limitations. What is worth doing is worth doing poorly or partially, if the alternative is not doing anything at all.

Being what I am, a creature of time and of flesh and blood, I have need of pacing myself in the good I would do. If I run like a fury for the first mile of a 10-mile race, and then collapse in a heap, I am not really a better runner than someone who is slower, but who gets there. Here we may adapt St. Augustine's observation that it is better to go slow on the right road than fast on the wrong one.

Mention of the idea of a "race" suggests another point about humility and its deadly enemy, pride. One of the characteristics of the vicious kind of pride (and there is a legitimate and honorable kind) is that it is grossly competitive. Such pride doesn't enjoy an achievement for its own objective worth, but because that achievement outshines somebody else's, or everybody else's. Thus the proud man is not proud of doing good but of doing better; of being rich but of being richer; of being smart but of being smarter; of being successful but of being more successful. The proud man thus eventually loses the capacity to delight in anything for its own sake, and to share with others in that delight. His competitive approach alienates him from others and from the objectivity of things. His gifts and accomplishments become walls instead of bridges.

Another point about humility. Because we are weak and flawed, because we are human and slow-growers, we can't wait until we are perfect before beginning to live. In this respect, the "better" can easily become the enemy of the "good." But, in point of fact, we don't solve our problems and then start living. We solve our problems by living. Hence, we have to learn to live with mistakes, failures and imperfections. As Father Eugene Kennedy puts the matter, we have a call to imperfection. For life is not an arena where no mistakes are to be made, but a laboratory where people make mistakes and learn from them.

Psychiatrist Leslie Farber makes a fascinating study of raw, unreal willfulness in his book, *The Ways of the Will*. What he says about the spiritual goals of Christians applies to any perfectionist goals which a man might set for himself: "Christians were enjoined to imitate Christ in the full knowledge that success was forever impossible. The blasphemy or despair issues not from the pursuit of impossible goals, but only from forgetting their impossibility, forgetting the difference between an ideal and a fact."

A man who cannot accept his own creaturely imperfection would find it hard to accept this viewpoint, or to understand Alfred North Whitehead's belief that the greatest boon to the human race has been the impractical ethics of Christianity.

As man relearns in modern times how limited his freedom is, and how many are the irrational forces working on him, theologians are stressing anew the idea of a theology of compromise. After all, how does a Christian obey the commandments and the beatitudes in their stark absoluteness, when even the just man falls seven times a day, when we lie if we say that there is no sin in us?

"Compromise" will sound like an ignoble word to some people. But there is a "promise" in "compromise." And the man who works sincerely at fulfilling the promise and utilizing present possibilities is not an unworthy disciple. Our human and Christian ideals are like those stars of the heaven, which we never reach in themselves, but by which we guide our course.

There is no denying how much evil and dishonesty exist in the world. A man who would concentrate on that fact alone would find more than enough to overwhelm and shatter him. If we bring to this fact of existence a perfectionistic attitude and an unhumble trust in the power of our own willfulness—even willfulness in the service of good—we will be heading for serious trouble.

History provides sobering examples of the way in which the fight against corruption can itself be infected by that very corruption. It also shows how overzealous expectations of speedy victory lead to discouragement and abandonment of the struggle. The motto of the late architect Mies Van der Rohe applies to more than architecture: "Less is more." The humble man will also understand another motto of this famous designer: "God is in the details."

These observations have a special contribution to make to those many idealistic young people in the world today who are determined to do something about age-old problems such as war, racism and poverty. These people need support and deserve it. One source of support is human, realistic attitudes toward the frustrations which lie in wait for those who are both idealistic and impatient. Even as President, with all the power of his office, John Kennedy admitted that his most painful discovery was how hard it is to get something done.

In his aforementioned book, Dr. Farber summarizes the dangers facing the idealistic: "Thus does our noble dream of perfection make cynics of us all, destroying our infinite variety, reducing us to our faculty for imitation, and rendering us despicable to ourselves." This dream can make us cynics by souring us on the whole enterprise of reform. It can destroy our variety by forcing on us one, prefabricated blueprint for instant success. It can make us carbon copies of the latest messiah who promises instant utopia. And it can make us hate ourselves because we will inevitably disappoint our own self-expectations.

Here then, in our unhumble and self-flattering dreams of human perfection, do we generate all sorts of monstrous pressures, inhuman pressures. As we grow enraged at what we cannot do, we create the gravest temptation of all—refusing to do what we actually can.

Humility: the willingness to be what you are and to do what you can. This is not a surrender to mediocrity, because one of the things you are is changeable, improvable, open to greater possibilities. And one of the things you can do 'is to move step by steady step toward greater maturity, greater inner freedom, more salutary impact on your environment.

THE FRENCH WRITER Gustave Thibon put into vivid imagery the heart of these ideas on humility and self-acceptance. I know of no better way to end these reflections than by citing his words:

"You feel you are hedged in; you dream of escape; but beware of mirages. Do not run or fly away in order to get free: rather dig in the narrow place which has been given to you; you will find God there and everything. God does not float on your horizon, he sleeps in your substance. Vanity runs; love digs.

If you fly away from yourself, your prison will run with you and will close in because of the wind of your flight. If you go deep down into yourself, the prison will disappear in paradise." ●

Many sublime values would disappear from life if there were no possibility of pain and suffering. Without such possibilities, where would courage be, or loyalty, or mercy?

"Cry. Cry if you must.
But do not complain.
The path chose you.
And in the end you will say,
Thank you."

6

Needed: A Philosophy
of Frustration

W HEN THE museum guards aren't noticeably
looking, people like to tap or knock on statues
— to see whether they are solid or hollow, whether
made of wood or stone or metal.

When a man is hit by frustration and suffering
he is in danger of revealing something deep about
himself. And it may be most of all to himself that
the revealing will be done. In his *Philosophical
Memoir*, the late Karl Jaspers went so far as to say
that "It is only in extreme situations that man becomes aware of what he is." What such situations
might be, Jaspers himself knew at firsthand from his
experience with the Nazis.

A man can read the daily paper or his own daily
heart and see that life is full of contradiction, frustration, adversity, failure, limitation, suffering and
absurdity. These ingredients are the cause of most
of the pressures every man must wrestle with. That's

why everyone needs a philosophy of pain, a philosophy of frustration.

What does such a philosophy provide? It gives a person a broad perspective for keeping individual wrestling matches in proportion. It provides him with a cushion of realistic expectations. It disposes him to become a master at drawing out the creative, humanizing possibilities which are part of every earthly frustration.

We don't have to agree with John Keats that "to think is to be full of sorrow and leaden-eyed despairs," but we can scarcely deny the encompassing role that such frustrations play in human lives. These painful frustrations range from the petty to the inexpressibly tragic.

We suffer from real evils and imaginary evils. We suffer not only from present pain, but from remembered pain and anticipated pain. We suffer our own pain; we can and should share the pain of others. We suffer in body, in mind and in spirit.

The mere fact that we greet each other day after day with the insistent question, "How are you?" is a comment on our changeability and vulnerability. This woundableness produced a profound pessimism in the ancient poet Sophocles and led him to say that there are but two blessings in life—never to have been born, or to have died young.

This same tragic sense suffuses one of the saddest and most beautiful stories I have ever heard. A father kept grieving and grieving for his lost son. "Why do you keep on weeping," asked his friends, "since it does no good?" The father answered: "That is why I weep, because all my weeping does no good."

Every man needs a philosophy of frustration. Each man must work out his own, to meet his own needs. Still, throughout history, men have tried to share what they have learned from their own suffering. For suffering is a pristine source of learning, though it often produces the kind of knowledge we think we would rather do without.

The ancient Greeks even linked their words *pathein* and *mathein* together and argued that to suffer (*pathein*) is to learn (*mathein*). There is a piece of English verse which spells out the same idea:

> I walked a mile with gladness and she chatted
>   all the way,
> But left me none the wiser for all she had to
>   say.
> I walked a mile with sadness, and never a word
>   said she,
> But, oh, the things I learned from her, when
>   sorrow walked with me.

If pain is a peerless teacher, we may be able to find in it some hint of an explanation as to why God allows it. Tears, they say, are good for the eyesight. They can help us see what is genuinely worthwhile, though we may have to do some losing before we get the point. This same thought was put graphically by one harried woman when she said: "A great tragedy can burn all the trash out of your life."

The French writer, Leon Bloy, made the same connection between sorrow and seeing when he wrote that a world without suffering would be a world without revelation. In the Temple of Jerusalem Simeon said to the mother of Christ: "Your own soul a sword shall pierce, so that the thoughts of many hearts may be revealed." Each man can decide what that sentence means, but it clearly links suffering with revelation.

The same Leon Bloy saw in pain a power even mightier than revelation. He saw in it the power of creation. Here are his unforgettable words: "There are in the heart of every man places which do not

81

yet exist. Pain must enter in before these places can come to be."

Another French writer, the philosopher Henri Bergson, put the problem of pain in a cosmic context when he said: "The universe is a machine for making gods." If God is love in some mind-shattering, mysterious way, and if it is true that it is no laughing matter to be loved by God, should we not expect to find in the human condition unique possibilities for the flowering of godlike qualities of love and goodness?

As Abraham Lincoln lay dying, an Army doctor sat steadfastly by his side and held the hand of the unconscious President. The doctor knew that the case was hopeless. But he also knew that the blinded victim might regain consciousness momentarily. Lest Lincoln experience even a second of sightless, solitary pain, the doctor sat hour after hour gripping the hand of the stricken giant.

What price could be put on that kind of compassion and greatheartedness? Mustn't we admit that many sublime values would disappear from life if there were no possibility of pain and suffering? Without such possibilities, where would courage be, or loyalty or mercy? Aren't such qualities, by their very nature, like "the tranquil blossom of the tortured stem"? Isn't love at its most magnificent when it is willing to sacrifice, to pay a price, to stand a loss? Wouldn't we all be fair-weather friends if there were no stormy weather?

The whole life of Jesus underscores this viewpoint. As he heads for the garden of agony and the subsequent cross, he tells his disciples: "That the world may know that I love . . . come, let us go from here." After his death he appears to two of his downhearted followers and insists that it was *necessary* for the Christ to suffer all these things and thereby enter into his glory, which is a glory of unbounded love.

It is against the background of ideas like these that a man can best raise the question as to whether the universe is basically good, basically malignant or basically indifferent. We can enjoy the wit of the man who said that this is the best of all possible worlds and everything in it is a necessary evil.

But when we ask about the goodness of the world we invoke the serious task of asking, "good for what?" It is obviously not good enough to be only a place where all day, every day, everybody can eat, drink and be merry. It is clearly not the work of a grandfather in heaven whose chief concern is to see that a good time is had by all — not even the best kind of good time which the best of men could imagine.

Is the world good? Is a blank crossword puzzle good? The puzzle is full of unfulfilled sections. Yet if the mastery of words is good, if the exercise of memory, patience and imagination is good, then the puzzle may well be good for its purpose.

You see a broken-down house full of flaws and aching for repairs. Is it good? It might be perfect for a movie producer or an artist who is looking for just that kind of house. A saint has said that God's meaning is love. As producer and artisan of the universe, a universe where some share of God's freedom is to be granted by him and taken seriously by him as a means for producing moral greatness, God may find the imperfect human condition perfect for his purposes.

It would be hard to deny that much of this world's evil comes from the bad use that men make of their own possibilities. Much of the trouble which afflicts "our proud and angry dust" is self-caused. We refuse to learn. We refuse to accept the laws of things and to learn from our mistakes. In an unnatural way we would be as gods making up our own definitions of good and evil. We want the easy way out.

But God seems to take our freedom much more seriously than we do. Imagine what would happen if we could rely on God to correct our mistakes and undo our sins immediately and directly. Would we ever learn? Would we ever become morally serious and responsible?

Look at the spoiled son whose wealthy and influential father bails him out of every jam. The father is actually ruining his son by sparing him the consequences of his own actions. Long ago Plato recognized that the worst thing that can happen to an evildoer is for his deeds to go unpunished.

Relatedly, if we could depend on God's doing what needed to be done, would we ever do anything difficult and maturing? This may be part of the answer to the question of the psalmist as to why God keeps his hand in his vest. God's tactics may be similar to those of a mother who lets her child bring a glass of water to a sick person in the house — not because the child can do it as well as the mother but because the child needs to learn consideration and helpfulness.

The poet Claudel saw a comparison between God withholding his hand at times and a father who is teaching his youngster to swim. At first the father will support his child upon the water. But if the son is to learn to swim by himself the parent must eventually withdraw his hand, even though the son may have to endure some panic and swallow a few mouthfuls.

Sometimes we are quite skillful at handling the major frustrations of life, but allow the lesser, everyday types to throw us. We would perhaps like to do away with all such resistances, forgetting that the

84

saber-toothed tiger died out because he became too powerful for any opposition. We need to keep in mind the procedure of the weight lifter. He wants to strengthen his muscles so he strains against weights which will truly give him an argument.

With respect to gaining knowledge, the philosopher Immanuel Kant used a picturesque example to make a similar point: "The light dove cleaving in free flight the thin air, whose resistance it feels, might imagine that her movements would be far more free and rapid in airless space." But, of course, the dove would be wrong, as Kant thought Plato was wrong in trying to master knowledge by traveling through the vacuum of pure ideas.

Describing how he composes music Igor Stravinsky notes that at first he has a moment of terror as he feels an infinity of possibilities facing him. For, if everything is permissible, if nothing offers any resistance, he cannot use anything as a basis for effort. But then he reassures himself that he has at his disposal definite notes and intervals, as well as weak and strong beats. He determines to sink his roots into this solid and concrete field, which has both limitations and inexhaustible riches.

This musical genius concludes: "In art, as in everything else, one can build only upon a resisting foundation: whatever constantly gives away to pressure constantly renders movement impossible. My freedom thus consists in my moving about within the narrow frame that I have assigned myself. I shall go even farther: my freedom will be so much the greater and more meaningful the more narrowly I limit my field of action and the more I surround myself with obstacles."

Other examples of this basic human point are to be found in the various sports which millions of human beings enjoy. Isn't it the essence of every sport that some rules, some limitations, are laid down and that skill is developed by the player who operates within these boundaries? Indeed, the champion gives evidence of his skill precisely by triumphing within the odds which the rules place against him. This "success despite" generates the excitement and delight of those who watch an evenly matched and expertly executed game. This line of thought led Robert Frost to say that writing poetry without any kind of structure is like playing tennis with the net down.

Some noble souls are stoic and uncomplaining about accepting their own crosses, but are baffled, bruised and depressed by the fact that so much suffering strikes at so many people who from every human point of view are innocent and undeserving. There is undeniably a staggering mystery here, a mystery which can tempt a man to deny God or to hate him, or a mystery which can humble and chasten his heart as a most convincing and piercing reminder that man's viewpoint, even at its loftiest, is not the measure of the universe.

I would hope that the thoughtful and sensitive person who is scandalized by "the evils which God permits" would at least not make the burden more intolerable than necessary by imagining "all the suffering in the world" — as though any one person were doing all the suffering. As C. S. Lewis pointed out, there may be 10 people with toothaches waiting in the dentist's office, but no one is suffering 10 toothaches.

The suffering which can come to one human being can be overwhelming enough. There is no point in letting our imagination present us with a picture of cumulative suffering which no one is actually undergoing. From this point of view, suffering that seems pointless and undeserved is just as much a mystery if only one person in all history suffered it as if everybody suffered it.

Fortunate the man who becomes convinced, like Martin Luther King, that undeserved suffering is redemptive. This thought should be no stranger to a Christian, since his whole religion is based upon that very conviction. Indeed, the very dimensions and quality of evil in the world have convinced some people that man is more than a blind, meaningless accident of colliding molecules in a mindless universe. Some awesome drama is going on in human existence, they are deeply persuaded, a struggle involving principalities and powers and intelligences. Thus it happens that while some minds find in absurdity an argument for atheism, others find in it a harrowing and humbling sign of some transcendent reality in whose presence one removes one's shoes.

After this concentration on pain and evil, we may need to remind ourselves that if evil exists and is a mystery, so does and so is goodness. We may need to remind ourselves in the words of Gerard Manley Hopkins that "good grows wild, has shades, is nowhere none." Thomas Carlyle has a reminder too: "The tragedy of life is not how much we suffer, but how much we miss."

What we should not miss are the actual, concrete opportunities we have to do something about the world's evils, even though we can't do everything, and even though we haven't solved the problem of evil intellectually. A seminarian friend of mine was all uptight about all the world's problems while he was in the seminary. He left to join the Peace Corps and wrote: "The 'big issues' in the world have really disappeared as I face the beautiful everyday problems of improving the milk output of a cow and getting rid of worms on the maracuza plants."

Our human task may be said to be this: not to solve the problem of evil, but to dissolve it — to do something creative and healing about it, even if the incompleteness of my effort proves that I am not a god. Only those who are doing something constructive about the world's evils are entitled to wonder whether they might not have earned the right to complain to God for allowing them.

As men face the various pressures of life, they can perform no finer task than to share with one another by word and by example their own philosophy of frustration. I would like to end these thoughts by citing three of my favorite embodiments of such a philosophy.

The first is from the Greek tragedian, Aeschylus, and was quoted by Robert Kennedy to a group of grieving Negroes on the night of Martin Luther King's assassination. Two months later it appeared on the memorial card at Kennedy's own funeral:

> Even in our sleep, pain that cannot forget falls drop by drop upon the heart, until, in our despair, and against our will, comes wisdom by the awful grace of God.

In his book, *Markings*, Dag Hammarskjöld alluded to the grace of suffering in these moving words spoken to his own heart:

> Cry. Cry if you must. But do not complain. The path chose you. And in the end you will say, Thank you.

The final citation is from Alan Paton's deathlessly beautiful book, *Cry, the Beloved Country*. After a tragic experience the old and gentle hero of the

88

book, a native South African clergyman, says with
stunning simplicity:

> Pain and suffering, they are a secret.
> Kindness and love, they are a secret.
> But I have learned that kindness and love can
>   pay for pain and suffering.   ●

*The most creative, healing
and human way for a man
to reckon with pressures
is by living in the present
with others, borrowing light
from the past, hope from
the future.*

*Awareness
plus the present moment
equals reality.
It's in this reality alone
that we will grow or wither,
for there is no other.*

7

Coping With the
Dark Hours

THE DIFFERENCE between theory and practice
is often a spacious one, and probably never more
so than when it comes to grappling with human pressures and sufferings. Intellectually we may have
carved out for ourselves a fairly impressive philosophy
of frustration. Yet when the pressure is on, our
theories may seem to provide us with rickety, almost
useless defenses.

Our heads may try to brace us with the words
of Shakespeare's Friar Laurence: "I'll give thee
armour . . . Adversity's sweet milk, philosophy, to
comfort thee, though thou art banished."

But our feelings may retort with Romeo:

"Hang up philosophy!

"Unless philosophy can make a Juliet,

"Displant a town, reverse a prince's doom,

"It helps not, it prevails not. Talk no more."

Not to be discouraged by Romeo's advice, I want

to talk some more about pain, frustration, discouragement, depression, suffering — all those human experiences which make up the whole range of difficult moments, from a passing cloud of the "blues" to the dark night of the soul. This time, however, I want to talk about practice rather than about theory, though there is bound to be some overlapping.

My main thesis is that the most creative, healing and human way for a man to reckon with pressures is by living in the present with others, borrowing light from the past and hope from the future.

Most of us, I suppose, go along most of the time rather peaceably. In general, we exemplify Lincoln's remark that people are about as happy as they make up their minds to be. In the movie version of *Billy Budd,* Billy puts the same idea the other way round when he tells the sinister Claggart: "People, I find, are about as lonely as they want to be."

There will be stormy episodes, of course. Some are rather brief. (Can you name the three most bothersome things in your life this time last year?) Other episodes can be lengthy, such as the period of adolescence, when we are shifting all sorts of gears, stripping a few in the process, and wondering whether our emotions will ever settle down again.

At times it may seem to an adolescent that his adolescence is a disease. But those who survive that season of life can speak this word of comfort — that it is a disease which in most cases eventually burns itself out. You cure it by surviving it. Those of us who have survived may tend to forget how reassuring we might be to an adolescent just by letting him know that we know what he is going through, and that survival is possible.

For whatever reasons, some people bear the burden of being almost always edgy and unsure of themselves. It's as though they are walking a tightrope, and don't know whether there is a net down below in the unfathomed darkness. Hence, they are mortally afraid of losing their balance, especially by being pushed off by other people who come too close.

Yet it's lonely on such a tightrope, and these people don't want to keep others totally away. So they are betwixt and between, wanting people farther away when they get close, and closer when they get far. They give off conflicting signals, and people who want to take them seriously can get exasperated, not knowing whether the signals mean come or go.

The sense of constant ache which these people suffer might be more graphically compared to the problem of a man who is holding onto a rope and is afraid to let go because he doesn't know what lies beneath him, if indeed there lies anything at all. He is torn between the pain of holding on and the fear of letting go.

What such a man might need more than anything else, certainly more than a lot of philosophizing, is some kind of a fall or a letting go which will teach him that he can indeed survive, that nature has equipped him with an ample net, a resilient net which will catch him and let him bounce back.

Often a man will not take the risk of learning this redeeming lesson until he has grown so weary and disgusted with worrying that he "lets go" in a kind of reckless despair. This despair may well liberate a therapeutic anger, an anger which inflates a substantial cushion and communicates that sense of supportive strength which is exactly what the man needs to experience.

Noting how frequently men have found a sudden serenity after they have hit the bottom of hopelessness, psychologist William James advised: "Give up the feeling of responsibility, let go your hold, resign the care of your destiny to higher powers, be genuinely indifferent as to what becomes of it all . . . . It is but giving your private convulsive self a rest, and finding that a greater Self is there."

Another type of ceaseless worrier is the man who feels that he must always be justifying his existence. He doesn't see this existence as fundamentally a gift. So he must be perpetually paying off his debt to life, planning everything in great detail, living excessively in the future or in the past, and renouncing the art of leisure and of enjoyment of the present.

The person who finds himself inclined to be worry-ridden, who carries about with him a cloud of free-floating anxiety which clings now to one fidget and then to another, should quietly and gently ask himself what advantages he may be unconsciously finding in his troubles. We laughingly speak of those who enjoy ill health. Thus one of the characters in Christopher Fry's play, *The Lady's Not for Burning,* announces with a sigh: "I should never be at peace if I thought I lacked anxiety."

What sort of advantages might a person find in being a problem case, in being accident prone, in being anxiety-ridden? Well, he may be giving himself a prefabricated excuse for any possible failures. After all, anyone as hard pressed as he is couldn't be expected to do his best. He also gains attention and sympathy, and may thus hope to hold onto the people who he fears might otherwise cease to notice or care about him.

Such a constant state of worry also gives a man an unhealthy kind of self-awareness, an assurance that he's still there, and perhaps a sense that he is not only greatly miserable, but miserably great, like some tragic hero. A need to be thwarted may be linked with a need for ego awareness. If I go up the down escalator I will undoubtedly run into more people and be made much more certain of my own ego than if I take the usual route.

Whether my problems and pressures are short-range or long-range, whether they are unconsciously self-caused or otherwise, what practical techniques can help me make the best of them, help me solve them or at least creatively endure them?

The first thing I can do is try to see whether my distress signals are trying to teach me something. Am I attempting to do too much, or to be something I am not cut out to be? Am I trying to pursue contradictory goals? Do I, for example, want to be unhealthily dependent on others, and yet treated with respect as an adult? Or do I want to be unhealthily independent and yet treated considerately as a part of the gang?

Is there some way that I am trying to run with the rabbits and hunt with the hounds? Psychiatrist Karen Horney thought that many Americans suffer special conflicts because they belong to a culture which simultaneously idealizes the man who cares about his brother and the man who climbs the rungs of success, even over other people's bodies.

At times the recipe for outwitting a cloudy mood is just to dig in and outwait it. These are the times when the best way "out" is "through." A man who is building a house would be foolish to pull up his roots and start elsewhere just because a cloud cover temporarily moves over his site.

This outwaiting isn't easy to do. In fact, doing nothing can be the hardest thing of all to do. A boy who is learning how to dive and who is trying just to let himself fall, hands first, can tell you how demanding it is to do nothing. Yet one of the supreme skills of life is the art of knowing when and how to practice "masterful inactivity."

Another art which needs cultivating is that of knowing how "to care and not to care." This art is a matter of touch and of a kind of finesse, and takes time to develop. The skater who wants to make progress has got to cut into the ice. But if he cuts in too deeply, he won't move at all. If I am to type this chapter, I have to make the keys hit the paper. But if any key hits too hard and gets stuck, it will block further progress.

These images call to mind a retreat I made under the famous American Jesuit, Gustave Weigel. He pointed out that the Spanish word which St. Ignatius used for the recommended virtue of "detachment" literally means "unstuckedness." We need to get involved in what we're doing, to be attached to the projects in our lives, but we should avoid getting "stuck" in any paralyzing or dead-ending way.

The value of this kind of "distancing" finds a parable in the act of reading. Our eyes have to be close enough to read the letters. But if we get too close, if our eyes are literally on the paper, we will be closer to the letters, but we won't be closer to the meaning.

This parable can also shed some light on the cult of "experience" which tempts some people. For it is not experience itself which counts, but capacity for experience and the ability to learn from experience. The psychopath has plenty of experiences, but he can't seem to learn from them. And some of his experiences may prevent him from having other, more valuable experiences, or from having any further earthly experiences at all.

Despite a reasonable detachment (whose exact formula every man must work out for himself), we must nevertheless concentrate our energies severely and seriously on the present moment. As one school of psychiatry puts it: Awareness plus the present moment equals reality. It is in this reality alone that we will grow or wither, for there is no other.

Spiritual writers speak of the sacrament of the present moment. The Scriptures say that God is not the God of the dead, but of the living. And the Lord's Prayer advises us to pray for our "daily" bread — not for a weekly or monthly supply. This point is reinforced by the Old Testament story of the manna, of which the Israelites were commanded to store up only one day's supply at a time. Sufficient for the day is the evil thereof, and the grace we need to master the evil. God has not promised us grace today to wrestle with tomorrow's worries.

I will never forget a fascinating stranger who once told me he had a horror of dying in bed. "Do you know why?" he asked. "Because I am not going to die in bed. Hence, for me dying in bed is a nothing. And there is no grace for a nothing, and that is why I can think of this eventuality only with horror." Whether or not he was correct about this specific matter, he was surely right that there is no grace for the handling of nothing. Even with God, "nothing" is impossible.

Our imaginations are the mischief-makers here. At times we are like a driver who in his imagination piles up all the stones he is going to encounter on a mountain road and makes out of them a barricade which his emotions find too high to hurdle. The fact is, of course, that he will indeed meet all these stones, but not all at once.

Or, to alter the picture somewhat, we can think of ourselves as driving a car along a dark and dangerous road. If we imagine the road half a mile ahead of us or just behind us, we can frighten ourselves by the thought that we are totally engulfed in darkness. But the fact is that we do have our headlights, and as we advance into the darkness we bring our own light with us. The only important step in our lives is the next one, and the only part of the road with which we must really deal is the section just in front of us. If we take the normal precautions to keep our batteries charged, we can rely on the fact that when the future becomes the present its darkness will be manageable.

This light-and-darkness imagery recalls for me two rules for living which I have found helpful through the years. One warns that we shouldn't turn out the lights to see how dark it is. Yet sometimes we add to our depression by switching off all the hopeful prospects which would actually lighten and brighten the present darkness.

The second word of advice leaped up at me in a needed moment from the writings of the English poet, Coventry Patmore. His words have stuck in my mind over the past 15 years and often transmitted an unusual kind of strength in wavering moments. His statement was: "We do not deny in darkness what has been revealed to us in light."

There are terrible moments and sometimes even weeks and months when all our certitudes seem to disappear, and we find ourselves bewildered and besieged. Still, we can realize that we are in darkness, and that this period does not represent our most creative and insightful possibilities. During the physical night, all the colors are drained from the world. From the evidence before our eyes we might wonder if the colors ever really did exist or could possibly return. But wise men know that if the sun goes down, the sun also rises.

That is why we shouldn't deny in the dark what has been revealed in the light. Sometimes by a sheer act of the will, and without any compelling logic at the moment, we must choose to believe in the memory of our illuminated selves as opposed to the pressing evidence of our darkened selves. Meantime we should get busy doing something optimistic, the quicker to prime the pump of revitalization.

If you have ever been severely depressed, you know that the worst part of such depression is the feeling and the fear that the depression will never end. The worst part of such a tunnel is the lack of light from the other end — the absence of hope.

In his invaluable book, *Images of Hope*, William Lynch stresses the need we all have of hopeful images. Often we must borrow these images from another person, a person we can trust and who helps us by his vital confidence in the possibilities of the future and in the power which waiting has to bring us release from a sense of entrapment.

Such a person often helps by first reassuring us that it is all right, it is acceptably human to feel periods of despair. There is a story about a depressed patient who seemed unable to be helped by his psychiatrist. Finally, the doctor himself frankly admitted his own feeling of despair at helping the patient. From that moment, the patient began to improve.

It seems that in his despair, the patient had felt totally alienated from the human race, the race which, apart from himself, seemed so energetic, purposeful, hopeful. When the doctor despaired, the patient at last had company and felt in healing touch with humanity again.

Images of Hope warns against the "absolutizing instinct," the all-or-nothing tendency to make a whole of the part. This mentality tries to take the manage-

99

able edges and borders off of things, and inclines to spill over into unqualified absolutes. For example, it fails to distinguish between those desires which are of their nature hopeless (e.g., that I should be radically other than I am, that life should not be life), and those wishes which are hopeful (e.g., that I may do better with what I am, with what life is). It interprets one or several failures as total failure. But the part is *not* the whole.

When the hopelessness of the one situation invades and infects the other, then we are in the danger of total despair. As a way of keeping the border on things, one doctor always used to ask depressed persons just exactly when their depression began. By getting his patients to name a time before and a time after, the depression lost some of its absolute, unbounded quality and became to that extent more human and manageable.

Try an experiment with yourself sometime when you are feeling painfully stretched out in all directions by the prospect of some overwhelming fear or problem. Deliberately change the setting of your imagination. Bring yourself back to the room you are actually in, to the day and the hour which it actually is. By changing your "image," you may almost tangibly feel your emotions shrinking back into endurable, manageable size and shape. If any of the ideas or images mentioned in this chapter brought you a sense of relief, you were experiencing the power of hopeful images to liberate your own hope. You were also experiencing the way that the hopefulness of one human being can enlarge another's possibilities at any given moment.

In recent times both philosophy and theology have been giving increased stress to the importance of hope. Theologians, for example, have been speaking of the

God in front of man instead of the God above man. They are recalling how, when God gave Abraham the mission to go into a strange country (as the future is unknown territory), He did not say, "Go," but "Come"; come, with Myself leading the way.

Philosopher Gabriel Marcel defines hope as the affirmation of the possibility of communion. He means that the hopeful man in the depths of his heart says "yes" to the possibility that no man need be locked hopelessly inside himself, but that the leapfulness of love empowers him to overcome all gulfs, even that of physical death, and to maintain a bond of communion with all that is loved and dear.

As modern as is the theme of hopefulness, we find very striking literary expressions of that theme in the writings of a man of yesterday, Charles Peguy. In one poem he depicts God as saying:

"You can ask a lot of kindness from man, a lot of charity, a lot of sacrifice . . . But what you can't ask of him, by gum, is a little hope. A little confidence, don't you know, a little relaxation, a little yielding, a little abandonment into my hands."

Elsewhere Peguy writes: "Faith is she who remains steadfast during centuries and centuries. Charity is she who gives herself during centuries and centuries. But my little hope is she who rises every morning . . . who every morning wishes us good day . . . who says how do you do to the poor and the orphan. Faith is she who watches during centuries and centuries. Charity is she who watches during centuries and centuries. But my little hope is she who goes to bed every night and gets up every morning and really sleeps very well."

Blessed is the man who knows how to hope and who has the imagination with which to help others to hope. Pope John was preeminently such a man.

A recent book tells of the cordial relationship between Pope John and an Italian Communist artist, Manzu.

One day, while Vatican II was still in the planning stage, John told Manzu: "I thought of you this morning. Someone asked me how we could answer all the questions which would be asked at the Vatican Council. I remembered your saying that you find your answer as you work, in the work itself, and I said: — 'Never mind, Monsignori, we will find our answers as we work in the Council, or afterwards as we apply it to the world.'"

This confidence in the future, in the unfolding of life itself, in the happily unexpected, such is the secret of the fruitfulness and the tranquility of the man of hope. There is no better way to eliminate unnecessary clouds and to creatively endure inevitable ones than the nurturing of this forgotten virtue.

"Do not look back in anger," goes a word of advice, "nor forward in fear, but around in awareness." This awareness of possibilities, fed by communion with other men, is the fountainhead of hope. Thus my man of hope, triumphing over the dark hours, lives in the present linked with his brothers, borrowing light from the past and courage from the potential of the times ahead. ●

*Love is our profoundest
destiny, our loftiest
possibility, our surest
source of happiness.
It's our I.D. card.*

*Love causes suffering, but
it's also a remedy for the
wounds it causes.
It's a way of seeing;
it's knowledge whose
roots are in the heart.*

8

People Who Need People

THE TRUEST, deepest, most important, most revealing and most astounding thing that anyone
can say about you is this: You are made to love and
to be loved. Love is your profoundest destiny, your
loftiest possibility, and your surest source of happiness. Love is your I.D. card and your passport to
human fulfillment.

That is why all of us are people who need people.
Yet one of the most illuminating indicators of the
human condition, of man's predicament and plight and
fractured status is that many of us find it so hard
to discover what love really is, and so hard to practice what love really means, and so afraid of what
love really does. It couldn't be stranger if fish were
afraid of the water and eagles were frightened by the
open sky.

And so we find ourselves understanding only too
well the famous words of Jean Paul Sartre—"Hell is

other people"; or even his less famous definition of a friend as someone who hates the same enemies as you do. We understand the literary character Dmitri Karamazov when he says that he would gladly die for the human race, but feels like strangling the man next to him who keeps sniffling. We know what Charlie Brown is going through when he confesses that he loves humanity but can't stand people.

Again and again we find that our pressure problems are actually people problems. No wonder we have problems when we want to love others and fear to love them, when we can't get along with them and can't get along without them, when we are angry with them and dare not show our anger, when we feel we must dominate them because we fear they want to dominate us.

The fact that most of our pressure problems and emotional problems are people problems is one reason why a psychiatrist is different from a book about psychiatry. A psychiatrist is a person, and when you are relating and reacting to a person, things start to happen. Memories stir, fears and needs are triggered, underground testing goes on, tender and hostile feelings surface, masks and disguises go into operation, and subtle transfers of energy take place.

But if people are our problem, they are also the solution to our problem. In general, a man is either moving toward people, away from people or against people. There will be problems and pressures connected with each of these situations. The main argument of this chapter is that the pressures of the first approach are supremely worthwhile; the rewards of that approach make all the troubles of being human tolerable.

The previous chapters in this book have in a sense been self-centered. We've talked about self-knowledge, the value of emotions, the handling of personal frustration, the importance of humility. Yet we have probed into ourselves in order to find how best to get outside ourselves. Getting hold of ourselves is a prerequisite for giving ourselves.

We have inspected the rocket of our nature carefully so that we can better make the journey out of our own atmosphere into orbit around others. There's this difference from mechanical rockets, though: We can't wait for perfection before blasting off—for in our very attempts to love we learn of our possibilities and deficiencies and are called upon to make in-flight corrections.

Moreover, some of the themes already touched upon shed precious light upon the meaning of love. For love is my humble willingness that the person in front of me should be what he is and become what he can. Love will cause suffering and frustration, but it is also the sole remedy for the wounds it causes. Love is a way of seeing; it is a knowledge whose roots are in the heart.

When I love you, I affirm you, I say yes to you, I acquiesce in your identity as other than me. Love is an appetite for the other—not an appetite which would consume you into myself, but a taste for the other precisely as "other." With such a taste, I delight in difference. My loving affirmation is like the salt that seasons—it doesn't make all things taste the same, but brings out the unique flavor of each. It is the sunlight which makes each thing radiate with its own color.

He who can rightly sense the searchless mystery of personhood knows that he is on holy ground when he stands in the presence of the other. If his ego can stand the threat of difference, he will take off the shoes of a crude selfhood which doesn't care about the other. If he sees the divine personhood blazing reflectedly in the other he will hear the call to universal reverence. Thus Mahatma Gandhi said: "He who would be the friend of God must either leave the world or make all men his brothers." Love, wrote Martin Buber, is the responsibility of an "I" for a "Thou," and this responsibility becomes crucifying for the man "who ventures to bring himself to the dreadful point of loving *all* men."

Hatred or indifference, by contrast, is a failure of the imagination. It sees the other as a stereotype, as one of a group, as a case, with all the mystery and unique identity pasted over by unimaginative labels. It sees the other as a problem rather than as a mystery. As a problem, the other is "out there," in front of me, totally graspable, totally outside of the mystery of myself, and hence able to be dealt with by technique, to be handled as an object that is rounded off and completely susceptible to manipulation.

There is one habit of mind which makes it easier for some of us to make objects out of other people. We look at another in his *role* as an adult, a parent, a teacher, a policeman, a clergyman. Then we take our idea of the essence of that role, and apply that idea severely to the performance of the person in question.

When it comes to ourselves, however, we may know what our role requires of us as a student, a grown-up, a Christian. But we take an "existential" point of view. That is, we take into merciful account all the excusing, concrete factors of our actual existence, for instance, that we come from an underprivileged family, that we have a headache or a toothache or some gnawing worry on our minds. In other words, we are essentialists with others and existentialists with ourselves.

There is a story about two traffic judges who both

got speeding tickets on their way to work, so they agreed to try each other's case. The first judge considered the good record of the defendant and decided to dismiss the case. Reversing places, the acquitted judge said that he would like to be lenient, but that there had been too many speeding cases lately, so he would have to fine the defendant and make an example of him. Thus a humorous example of the double standard.

Christians know they are commanded to love their neighbor, even though this isn't the same as liking your neighbor or being in love with him. True, liking is a matter of feeling and taste, reactions which are not entirely under our conscious control. Still, we might envy Will Rogers in his statement that he never met a man he didn't like. It seems to me that the more we come to accept ourselves and to give approval to ourselves in our limitations, the less threatened we will be by others, and hence the more serenely we will be able to see their good points.

Happy the man who believes that "to know all is to forgive all." If this saying as a universal statement is an exaggeration, at least it is a noble one. To the extent that it is true, it summons us to use our imaginations and to exercise our capacity for empathy —feeling with others. The old Indian advice holds true: "Don't criticize a brave until you have walked for a week in his moccasins."

Loving others in such an imaginative, affirmative way will help us to like them, with increased benefits to both sides. For such loving will generally put people at ease and encourage them to show their better selves.

Think of those persons in your life who have approached you from the start as though they were already your friend. Chances are you were inclined to respond in a friendly way. By acting as though you were already a friend, they made you friendly. This situation is similar to the way that grown-ups talk to a child as though the child can understand, and by this procedure they actually bring the child to understand. Theologians sometimes say that God does not love us because we are good, but rather that we are good because he loves us and to the extent that we let him love us.

When a person feels this divine initiative to be true in his own case, when he experiences a sense of gratitude for a free gift from God, he will feel inspired to "go and do likewise." He will then be undertaking membership in God's "special forces"—the people who go out of their way to love the unlovely, to befriend the friendless and to give the thankless something to be thankful for.

If you hear the call to such a challenge, you might exercise your empathy and imagination on the groups of human beings who are on the "outs" from the point of view of any "in" group—such as hippies, dropouts, militants, Communists, homosexuals: all the rejects of our own society.

There is a beautiful remark in the Jewish Talmud which is applicable here: "He who cares for his own child is like a stream which nourishes a tree along its banks. But he who loves another's child is like a cloud which goes from the sea into the desert and waters there a lone and lonesome tree." At a time when American society is being fragmented into so many hostile "in" groups and "out" groups, the disciple of Christ has no more urgent and timely task than to help break open closed circles. Edward Markham put the program well:

> He drew a circle which shut me out
> As a heretic, rebel, a thing to flout;
> But love and I had the wit to win:
> We drew a circle that shut him in.

Incidentally, to love such "outcast" people or any person "for the love of God," is not really to love them for some accidental reason outside themselves. To see and to revere in another the "image of God" is to see a value and a possibility which is identical with that person's deepest self. For it is the highest act of God's creative power that he can create an image which has its own inner identity and existence, its own freedom. Here is the very paradox of God's causality with respect to human nature: God causes, yes. But he causes a man to be free. Hence, to love another as God's image or for the love of God is at the roots to love a person for himself.

In the misuse of his freedom, or sometimes in the absence of mature freedom, a person may quite successfully bury his lovable features. God's image may grow tarnished indeed. Here there is need of an expert, a man who can believe in and conspire with that person's better possibilities. In his novel, *The White Stone,* Carol Coccioli has one of his characters say: "Charity means to see Jesus in others, without expecting them to act like Jesus."

The fruitfulness of such charity is suggested by the story of a Byzantine emperor who was inspecting his palace shortly after he came into power. In a remote part of his dwelling he found on the pavement a marble stone with a cross marked on it. It was not right, thought the emperor, that men should walk upon the cross. So he ordered the stone to be removed. But beneath this stone the workmen found a similar stone. Once again the emperor ordered it removed.

111

This process continued until a great treasure was found buried beneath the spot. In their dealings with others, Christ's most ingenious disciples refuse to "walk" on other people, signed as they are with the cross of Christ, and they thereby help to bring hidden treasures to the surface.

These basic ideas about love help to put the mystery of sexuality into perspective. There can be love without sex, and sex without love—at least with respect to the genital expression of love. Genitality can be one special way of expressing love, but it need not be so. Just as our organs of speech can be used to help or to harm, so our sexual organs can be used to express a gift, but also to degrade, to dominate, to manipulate, to avenge.

There are critics of Sigmund Freud who agree that he was right to link personality disturbances with sexual disturbances, but who feel that he misread the link. Whereas he inclined to blame personality disturbances on sexual disturbances, it seems more likely that sexual disturbances are a reflection of personality disturbances. In this view, it is not sexuality which explains personality, but the other way around.

Eric Fromm has made two points on this whole subject which have proved especially enlightening to me. He warns against the notion that if I find the right person, I will automatically be able to love him properly. Rather, Fromm sees mature loving as a capacity for giving, a capacity which is no more instantly created by discovering the right person, than the art of swimming depends simply on discovering the right body of water. Success in this area, then, depends more on my being the right person than on my meeting the right person. Which is not to deny that meeting the right person can help me become the right person. For we not only want to be loved, but to be worthy of being loved.

Fromm also warns that the strength of my feeling for another person is not necessarily a sign of how deep my love is. It may rather be a sign of how intense my loneliness was before I met this person. In any case, authentic love is a response to a real person, a person who is not just a reflection of an inner self to which I am clinging in a narcissistic, self-infatuated way.

Trouble often arises in a marriage when one partner discovers that the other partner is truly "other," and not just a projection of his own self, nor just a rigidly needed stereotype of a little child who desperately needs him, nor an all-competent parent whom he desperately needs. A happy couple give to each other out of the abundance of their maturity. An unhappy couple latch onto each other out of the desperations of their own immaturity. This distinction highlights the difference between loving a person because you need him, and needing a person because you love him.

Someone once wrote a book entitled *Love is Enough*. A reviewer started his review with two simple words: "It isn't." Mature love recognizes its own limitations. There are some dragons which a man must slay within himself. The love which another brings to me can encourage me to enter alone within myself and slay those dragons. It can convince me that I can slay them, and give me the motivation to do so. But another's love can never do the job for me. Some people spend many years looking fruitlessly for such a love, and they are bound to be disappointed.

If we are to learn about love and grow in it, we have need of some close friends. Is it a widespread human fear that if someone knows us he won't love us, and if he loves us he doesn't know us? In any case, friends are for knowing you and loving you anyway.

On the subject of friendship, St. Augustine coined one of his most perceptive phrases, a phrase whose depth modern phenomenology has rediscovered. Said Augustine: "Nothing is friendly to a man without a man who is a friend." The whole universe can take on a hostile inhuman meaning to the man who is truly friendless. He who has a friend, however, has the potential of discovering a human meaning and giving a human response to the whole universe.

MARTIN BUBER speaks of man's instinct to make everything into a "Thou." If this instinct is mankind's truest, if behind every particular Thou lies the absolute Thou, then everything may well depend on a single Thou of friendship in our lives.

I would like to conclude by mentioning a few qualities which promote the essential work of love. I think of the attribute of "courtesy"—a word related in its origin to the idea of a court, a royal court, where good manners reflect the presence of the king and the bond which links his courtiers together. John Ruskin had an honorable standard on this score: We must be consciously kind to all or we will be unconsciously unkind to some.

I think of the quality of "tact"—a word which in its roots refers to the sense of touch. We do not grab a bird the way we grab a baseball bat. We don't touch a champagne glass the way we touch a frying pan. If we know how to tune in to the uniqueness of the other person, we can develop the art of knowing when to say what, and how. It was such tact which led Jesus to say to his disciples: "I have other things to say, but you cannot bear them now."

Gratefulness or, more precisely, the expression of

114

gratefulness is another characteristic which manifests and multiplies love. You can probably recall quite vividly the times when another person took the time and effort to show you his gratitude, even by a brief letter or some small gift. Such memories testify to the power of gratefulness, and are a helpful reassurance that you are not being taken for granted.

The neglect of such seemingly small gestures, such as saying "please" and "thank you," can contribute eventually to large losses. Edna St. Vincent Millay put the danger well when she wrote:

> 'Tis not love's going that hurts my days,
> But that it went in little ways.

For many people Pope John embodied in a most simple but compelling way these qualities of courtesy, tact and gratefulness. For me, one incident demonstrated with the brilliance of genius the kind of man these qualities produced. When Pope John overcame nervous objections and received in audience the son-in-law of Russian Premier Khrushchev, he ended the interview with this magnificent remark: "They tell me, sir, that you are an atheist. But surely you will not forbid an old man to send a blessing to your children."

It was this Holy Father's lifelong ideal to see across every barrier the face of a brother. This ideal recalls a favorite story which will serve well to end these words on the endless subject of love.

An ancient rabbi once asked his pupils how they could tell when the night had ended and the day was on its way back.

"Could it be," asked one student, "when you can see an animal in the distance and tell whether it is a sheep or a dog?"

"No," answered the rabbi.

"Could it be," asked another, "when you can look at a tree in the distance and tell whether it is a fig tree or a peach tree?"

"No," said the rabbi.

"Well, then, when is it?" his pupils demanded.

"It is when you can look on the face of any man and see that he is your brother. Because, if you cannot do this, then no matter what time it is, it is still night." ●

*Why are there so many
vivacious and brilliant
children and so many dull
adults? The loss of the
sense of wonder has something
to do with this decline into
dullness.*

*At every stage of growth we
have to give up an old
security and accept a new
risk, a new challenge. If we
don't we'll decay, we'll in
some way die.*

9

Wonder and Delight

LOOKING BACK over the years, I find that there are two human emotions which are deeply nourishing, closely related and hard to keep in good working condition. They are eminently worth working at because they help considerably to keep human life human. Which means that they assist a man in living creatively with pressure.

These emotions are wonder and delight. For various reasons it may be practically impossible to keep your life wonder-ful and delight-ful. But it is also quite possible for a man's life to become almost totally drained of these enriching qualities. The battle then is to cultivate the habits which encourage these experiences to occur and to grow.

The earliest philosophers recognized that philosophy itself begins with wonder. If the philosophy is vital, it will end there too. (For the eighth wonder of the world should be anybody who thinks there are only seven.) At issue here is not only philosophy in a technical sense, but that philosophy of life by which a person lives.

To wonder is to recognize that you are in the presence of mystery, in the presence of a reality which is a curious combination of light and darkness. To the extent that a mystery is dark, it is not a wall against which you bash your head but a well from which you draw new draughts of insight and refreshment, but which you find you can never really exhaust.

Here I am not talking only about "mysteries" in the theological sense of some divine revelation. I am talking about every aspect of the universe in which man finds himself. Most of all I am talking about man himself, man the ceaseless questioner, the creature in whom creation becomes aware of itself. A humorous limerick emphasizes this unique role of man the unraveler:

> A life-force afflicted with doubt
> As to what it was bringing about
> Cried: "I am blind
> But I'm making a mind
> Which may possibly puzzle it out."

One human question which needs puzzling out is this: Why are there so many vivacious and brilliant children and so many "dull" adults? The loss of the sense of wonder surely has something to do with this decline into dullness. Rabbi Abraham Heschel noted recently that the worst of sins is to take the earth for granted. Children have not learned to commit that sin. True poets likewise fight against that discourtesy toward reality.

Why do we lose the sense of wonder? Among the reasons these two strike me as the most influential:

120

First, a man's pragmatic, practical-minded self begins to focus almost exclusively on the "useful" aspect of things. Less and less does he ask in a kind of pure openness and curiosity: What is this reality in front of me? Rather, more and more he wants to know: What is this thing for? Which means: What's in it for me? What can it do for me to heighten my power and comfort? How can I twist it, turn it, manipulate it, change it into something more valuable on the marketplace?

Not only does practical man limit his interest to the functional aspects of reality. Brainy man inclines to limit himself to the "classification" of reality. He puts things into groups and categories and easily overlooks or desensitizes himself to what is unique and individual about each item in a group of similar items.

This logical, categorizing and "essentialistic" approach to reality is linked up with the scientific method and approach—a valid approach in its own right. But what we tend to forget is that there is no science of the individual. Uniqueness is, in a very profound sense, unspeakable—because all our words are group words. If I call Fido a dog, or a German shepherd, or "mine," I am in each case locating him in a group to which other individuals belong. For purposes of distinguishing Fido from all other dogs I can further describe him by means of a perhaps unique collection of adjectives—"fat, brown, one-year-old, a scar on the left ear"—but each of these is itself another group word.

The poet Edwin Arlington Robinson once said that in God's vocabulary there are no adjectives. By this remark he meant to distinguish human knowledge, which is so partial, superficial and groupy, from divine knowledge, which he saw as a total and penetrating grasp of the specialness, the uniqueness of each individual thing. Every poet himself is godlike to the extent that he tries to celebrate the freshness and unrepeatability of a person or event. He can thus be called the scientist of the particular. For his part, Cardinal Newman felt that Christianity imposes on a man such a poetic view of reality.

Scientist William G. Pollard, executive director of the Oak Ridge Institute of Nuclear Studies, recently pointed out that a chief characteristic of 18th- and 19th-century science was a sense of demolishing mystery. Nature's secrets were being unlocked, and hopes arose that one great formula would be found to explain everything.

"But," he continues, "the prevailing note in the expressions of opinion of the great scientists of our century underscores the openness of science. . . . We find the reintroduction of mystery at a very profound and deep level. . . . In every area of scientific investigation each new discovery, each resolution of some new question or mystery, simply leads to a larger number of other problems and further questions."

The sense of wonder of which I speak, however, is not in any case limited to those aspects of reality which science can usefully make predictable in terms of a mathematical explanation. Thus as a child I might have wondered how thunder is caused. Science gives me an "answer" and (unfortunately) my wonder may cease.

Science can indeed give me a certain kind of explanation and can satisfy a certain kind of curiosity. (Even then, according to Austrian physicist Ernst Mach, "when we think we have succeeded in understanding a process, what has happened is that we have referred unfamiliar incomprehensibilities to familiar incomprehensibilities.") But the wonder that anything exists at all, the wonder that I now exist and am able

122

to wonder: This is the kind of wonder which knowledge only serves to deepen in many sensitive minds. For such people Edwin Arlington Robinson's words hold true:

> . . . not the faintest or the farthest whirled
> First atom of the least that ever flew
> Shall be by man defrauded of the touch
> God thrilled it with to make a dream for man
> When Science was unborn.

This science, for instance, can give me all sorts of useful and true information about someone I love. Thanks to X-rays and other ingenious equipment, it can tell me about my beloved's blood pressure, lung conditions, basal metabolism, genetic structure, and so forth. But all such data leave undimmed (if they do not actually magnify) the central mystery of the other person in his baffling uniqueness.

What I am finding deficient here is not science as such, the scientific method, nor, least of all, scientists themselves. Hear the words of an indisputably great modern scientist: "The most beautiful thing that we can experience is the mysterious. . . . He to whom this emotion is a stranger, who can no longer pause to wonder and stand rapt in awe, is as good as dead: his eyes are closed. . . . To know that what is impenetrable to us really exists, manifesting itself as the highest wisdom and the most radiant beauty, which our dull faculties can comprehend only in their most primitive forms—this knowledge, this feeling is at the center of true religiousness." Thus Albert Einstein.

The object of my criticism is a certain narrow-mindedness which "science" seems to foster in some people. This mentality gives importance to and pays attention to only a part of reality: the functional or classifiable part. It loses contact with the uniqueness of things, the thing in itself, in its entirety. And this is where a person betrays himself—because he himself is individual, mysterious, more than merely functional, not totally classifiable.

A man, then, who is alienated from mystery and wonder is alienated from himself. How can he prevent or overcome this estrangement? Among the requisites is the recovery of a certain way of seeing and hearing. Chesterton said that you have to look at familiar things until they become strange. Putting that thought in another way, he noted that when you look at something for the 100th time, you are in danger of seeing it for the first time.

In this connection, there is a story about a lady who one day walked into a tree. She later explained that although she had seen the tree, she hadn't *realized* it. We use that word *realize* at times to mean "make real"—as when we realize our ambitions. There is a sense in which we must make things real to ourselves by letting ourselves experience the fact that they are real.

The poet Walter de la Mare provided a formula for the kind of vision I'm recommending. He wrote this advice: "Look your last at all things lovely every hour." If we all knew that at noon tomorrow every flower would disappear from the universe forever, some of us might actually look closely at any available blossom for the first time in years. In this spirit, a student of mine once wrote an essay about an autumn trip to the mountains where, he said, he witnessed the sole performance of October 16, 1967.

Really looking, really listening, really paying attention: These are skills which are seemingly a natural part of childhood, probably because a child hasn't grown "practical" enough to limit his gaze to what is functional about a thing, nor rationalistic enough to suppose that he has said all there is to say about a thing when he has classified it with similar things. Such attentiveness requires an exercise of reverence toward reality, an openness, a zone of interior silence where static won't jam out the messages of meaning being emitted by things. It requires a contemplative, listening, watching attitude against which the noise, the speed and the agitation of so much modern living make constant war.

SOMEONE ONCE ASKED an artist why he painted trees, inasmuch as God had already made so many. "Because," replied the artist, "you don't look at God's trees." By taking the tree out of the forest, isolating it and putting it within a frame on the wall, the artist hoped that some viewers might really see a "tree" for the first time in a long time.

Many benefits flow from this kind of seeing and listening. One was cited by the poet Gerard Manley Hopkins—"There lives the dearest freshness deep down things." This invigorating and refreshing freshness is the reward of those who can sufficiently turn down the volume of their own selfhood so that they can hear what other persons and things are really trying to say.

The refreshment, nourishment and delight which come to the man of wonder are importantly related to a person's whole growth. Centuries ago, Thomas Aquinas pointed out that "no man can live without delight, and that is why a man deprived of joy of the spirit goes over to carnal pleasures." His remark provides a key insight into many a person's emotional problems.

Many of these problems—persistent discouragement, depression, loneliness, a hounding sense of failure, feelings of inferiority, scrupulosity, obsession with sexuality—can be traced to a common cause: We are starving our personalities. By depriving ourselves of the richer kinds of delight we force ourselves to go scavenging for less wholesome kinds.

These unwholesome and damaging pleasures are not necessarily lustful, alcoholic, narcotic or gluttonous. They may be more subtle and more poisonous. Thus the poet Gerard Manley Hopkins speaks of "the carrion comfort of despair." And Thomas Merton many years ago referred to the same lethal diet as "the rotten luxury of despair."

In other words, there exists a dangerous kind of delight in melancholy, in self-pity, in being a problem. At first we may neither intend nor foresee the trouble which this kind of self-indulgence will inflict on ourselves and on others. But just as the unwanted hangover is the result of the wanted intoxication, so the laws of personality disorder will have their own inevitable effect once they are put into operation.

For there are definite laws of personality growth and personality withering. These laws work whether or not we understand them. They automatically operate against us if we either willfully defy them or thoughtlessly neglect them. The two following illustrations offer, I think, helpful clues to these laws of personality.

Think of the human personality as a deep mountain lake fed by outside sources of water. Beneath the lake surface a number of crags lie submerged. Our conscious life is like a boat operating on the surface of the lake. As long as the water supply is maintained, the boat is safe from the dangers below. But if that supply is seriously diminished, the boat runs the risk of "cracking up" or of having its joyful activities sharply curtailed for fear of "cracking up."

126

This picture highlights the fact that every normal person has "crags" in his makeup. A man shouldn't be frightened to find that occasionally these crags will appear through the churning waters of some emotional strain. He need only reassure himself that the laws of supply are also real. There are definite and available ways for a man to keep his water level abundantly safe.

A well-known contrast in the Holy Land affords another illustration of these same laws. The Sea of Galilee and the Dead Sea are the two main bodies of water in that small country. Both seas are fed by the same source, the River Jordan. Yet they differ like night and day. The Sea of Galilee is brimming with life and beauty. The Dead Sea is just that—dead.

How explain the difference? For each particle of water which the Sea of Galilee takes from the north, it gives up one at the south. Thus as the Jordan flows through it, it lives because it gives. The Dead Sea, however, is locked within itself. It takes but does not give, and so it dies.

These two seas are like a geographical parable for Jesus' words: "He who saves his life will lose it; but he who loses his life for my sake will save it." Agnostic though he was, the poet A. E. Housman deemed these words to be the most profound moral wisdom ever uttered. It is amazing how many ways these words apply. At every stage of growth we have to give up an old security and accept a new risk, a new challenge.

If we don't grow we will decay. ("He who's not busy being born is busy dying.") If we try to save our lives, to protect ourselves too cautiously, we will in some way die. In the words of one psychiatrist: "The lack of courage to accept injury, and the incapability of self-sacrifice belong to the deepest sources of psychic illness. All neuroses seem to have as a common symptom an egocentric anxiety, a tense and self-centered concern for security, an inability to 'let go.' "

Daily life affords many examples of the necessity of living by giving, of growing up by giving up. The unborn child must eventually give up the security of the womb or else it will die. Later on the child will be able to walk only if it is willing to give up the slow security of crawling and to accept, with some bruises, a harder but better method of travel. No man can experience the deep satisfactions of maturity until he is ready to forgo the relative irresponsibility of youth. C. S. Lewis embodied this law of life in a witty epigram: "You can't just go on being a good egg. You must either hatch or go bad."

These various examples serve to dramatize the point that we may be starving ourselves out of growth and into many problems. We should never forget that life will nourish us if we give ourselves trustingly to it. That is why St. Paul tells us to do all that we do "from the heart." If we give our heart to whatever appropriately occupies us, these things in their own turn will give us heart. If we open ourselves generously to what life brings us, we will continue to grow day by day, and will be enriching ourselves with those rightful delights and satisfactions which result from being "real."

The trouble is we do too many things halfheartedly. We withhold our enthusiasm from life because we are too afraid of failing or of being hurt or of being disappointed. We cease bothering when we don't get the applause or gratitude we thought we needed. We fish instead of swim in the stream of life. We touch persons with only the tips of our souls. We don't sink the straw in far enough to get the satisfaction which lies beneath the foam.

The results are predictable. If we sever our supply line with realities outside ourselves, if we retreat into a safe but barren shell, then we will starve our emotions, diminish our delights and create a personality vacuum. As always, nature hates a vacuum. Therefore our darker instincts, our irrational needs and fears will rush in to fill up the emptiness.

Not realizing this law of the vacuum, many people waste their energy trying to empty their lives of worrisome things when they should be busy filling their lives with wholesome things. You don't solve your emotional problems and then start living. You solve them by living in a more deeply satisfying way.

That's the reason for the necessity of delight. The man who maintains his capacity to wonder at the realities which surround him will be keeping himself open to the delights of being lovingly in touch with the real. Such delights, which will often be as quiet and unnoticed as breathing, won't take all the pain and sorrow out of a man's life. But they will make the pain and sorrow worthwhile and much more humanly tolerable and creative. ●

Ours is a world where
revolutionary changes are
taking place, where any man
who takes the Gospel
seriously has special problems
and special opportunities.

Viewed as a mystery to be
lived rather than as a
problem to be solved, life
will provide the answers to
its own questions, though
not necessarily in the form
we are expecting.

10

Hoping to Lose

"TELL THEM what you're going to tell them. Tell them. Tell them what you've told them." So went a piece of advice I once heard about giving sermons. Another pithy rule of thumb, one which sounds less potentially boring, offered this proposal: "Be clear, be colorful, be seated."

This series of reflections is about to be seated. Since the telling has been spread over several chapters, it may be especially serviceable if I try here to sum up and round out the central ideas which the previous chapters have proposed for the task of becoming human and staying human in the fiercely pressurized world of today. It's a world where truly revolutionary changes are taking place in dizzying numbers and at dizzying speed. It's a world where any man who takes the Gospel seriously has special problems and special opportunities.

I've deliberately geared these thoughts away from

theological theory. There's something to be said for the likelihood that Christians are oversupplied with theory and controversies about theory. In any case, it's at the personal, practical, daily-life level that even the best theory has to work or fail. And that's where most of us have trouble.

Furthermore, lived experience—the actual flavor of wrestling with human problems as a conscious human being—is one of the best yardsticks for judging the value and the relevance of any development which a man is called upon to foster or resist. President Kennedy's ideal was that one man can make a difference, and every man should try. And he should try to be right.

Over many developments, of course, we have no direct control. In India they have a saying that you can't change the weather but you can change your attitude toward the weather. That's why there was a double focus to these articles: How best to remedy soluble problems? How best to live with insoluble ones? The wisdom to know the difference will come, I am confident, from living out the tested ideals I've been recommending.

In one sense, these ideals boil down to three: Know yourself, accept yourself, involve yourself. These three steps do not get themselves achieved in any neat sequence. The self we need to know and ought to accept is a self which will become clearer as it gets involved. I can sit on the side of the pool for weeks and theorize about the various possible relationships between my body and a body of water. But until I get in the swim, I'll never really learn the key, relevant questions.

The German thinker Goethe put the matter this way: "How can we learn to know ourselves? Never by reflection, but by action. Try to do your duty and you will soon find out what you are. But what is your duty? The demands of each day." I'm not so sure about that *never* of reflection, unless he meant reflection in a vacuum. But his general thrust is one which is confirmed by much experience.

A program of knowing, accepting and involving yourself will call into instant play the capital suggestions of these articles. They will reassure a man that it is all right to be human, to be confused, to suffer limitations, to have all sorts of feelings, none of which he "ought not" to feel. They will make a man more at peace with the rich resources of his emotionality. They will promote his willingness to be what he is and to do what he can. Negatively, they will spur the growth of an adequate philosophy of frustration and of the practical skills for enduring the terrible hours. Positively, they will feed his ability to love, to wonder, and to take delight.

A picture on a friend's wall shows a man walking through the woods with his youngster and a dog. The caption reads: Take the time. God knows that such taking isn't easy for masses of people today. There's a story about a teacher who took her students to a museum and announced: "Now, don't start looking at the exhibits, or we'll never get finished." Another story tells of a group of natives who were being pushed too fast on a safari. Finally they rebelled and sat down on the trail, waiting (as they said) until their souls caught up with their bodies.

Like people thumbing through an illustrated cookbook, we have perhaps so many choices today that we stir our imaginations to the point of paralyzing our hands. If we become mere hurried tasters at life's automat, we will deprive ourselves of the refreshment of balanced, humanized meals. We can even become ontological gluttons, and get spiritual indigestion by trying to cram in too much reality at one time. Like

133

trying to listen to two symphonies at the same time. Or playing a 33⅓ rpm record at the 78 speed, to save time.

Take the time. Don't be forever dashing. Try sauntering. The word "saunter" has an instructive background. It's from the French "Sainte Terre," Holy Land, and refers to the easy pace taken by the pilgrims who were enjoying the trip itself as well as relishing the goal. Life itself is a holy land, and deserves to be enjoyed en route. (Gilbert and Sullivan, by contrast, caught the spirit of much modern mad motion in a song which says: "If you ask the special function of this never-ceasing motion, we reply without compunction that we haven't any notion.")

The word "holy" too has an illuminating family history. It's from a root Anglo-Saxon word meaning unwounded and unharmed, hence all there, hence "whole." Thence we get the words "heal" (make whole), "healthy," "hale" (and hearty) and even the greeting "hail" (be whole). Recall the words of Eugene O'Neill cited earlier: "Man is born broken . . . God's grace is glue." Holiness, then, is truly wholeness. Whatever makes or keeps a man wholly human—the theme of all these articles—is truly a work of holiness, a godly thing.

Some people seem to ease their way gracefully from one stage of growth to another. But many of us find that growing is a matter of growing pains; and sometimes it feels as though it's the pains which are growing. Psychologically, the process will take this form for many: At each stage we finally achieve some kind of coherent pattern of meaning and of values. Then, if we are truly alive, we undergo new experiences which don't fit into the old pattern. Gradually or suddenly, we feel the old pattern breaking down and we spend a greater or lesser time in a harrowing

134

kind of no-man's-land, while a new and better pattern is trying to emerge and solidify.

Here is an instance of the need for waiting, for just vegetating trustfully in the hope that something valuable is happening which will more than make up for the pain. The situation is similar to the state of a hard crab which has sloughed off its shell and is undergoing a vulnerable soft-shell status for a while. That vulnerability, by the way, is enough to make a person "crabby." Fortunate the man who finds sympathy and support from family and friends while he is in this touchy condition.

I've spoken already about the essential role of the imagination in the task of handling the future and weathering the touchy times. One of my theology teachers used to speak of the imagination as the fool of the house. That's only half the truth. For the imagination can be also the king of the road. Don't identify the imagination with the imaginary, at least not in the sense of what is fictitious and hopelessly unreal. The future is, to be sure, unreal in one sense. But we have the power to make what is presently unreal real in the future. And that "unreality" can be something better or something worse. In a positive, creative sense, imagination can be defined as the capacity to envision possibilities and work toward them.

The trouble is that we often limit ourselves to imagining depressing possibilities or concentrating on the impossibilities. We're like the pessimist who, facing the choice of several evils, takes all of them. Sometimes, like a stuck slide projector, we take a given bad situation and cast its grim dispiriting colors and shapes onto the future. The result is that we sadden ourselves, freeze our hopeful energies, and blind ourselves to the beckoning of better things. The future is like a white screen capable of taking on a multitude of possible forms. Yet in our rage and depression we can turn against the screen, when the trouble lies within our own projecting equipment.

Among some people, it is fashionable to belittle ideas like "the power of positive thinking," "psychocybernetics," and Coué's recommendation that a man keep telling himself: "Every day in every way, I'm getting better." No doubt, such techniques are shallow if they aim solely at external, material success, or if they are divorced from hard, productive action and degenerate into a falsely cheery kind of autosuggestion.

Yet even such distortions and trivializations draw their persuasiveness from genuine facts about the role of the imagination and of hope in human development. This development is not separate from sorrow and tragedy—indeed, it often presumes them. Maria Trapp's conviction that God never closes a door without opening a window is a deep and valid affirmation of the hopefulness of life in its gift of authentic value choices in every human situation, no matter how externally limited and unchangeable.

As chaplain of a children's home, I used to tell the youngsters that life is hard by the yard but a cinch by the inch. What I wanted to fight was their understandable tendency to imagine the future in terms of their scarred pasts. I wanted to liberate their possibilities by having them focus their energies on the manageable demands and promises of each present moment in their lives. It has been gratifying to have a number of these youngsters tell of the good effect which the unsophisticated wisdom of this maxim has had on them during their stormier moments.

Throughout his life, a man may have to keep telling himself during his stormier moments that "the part is not the whole," that "something is better than

136

nothing," and that "this too will pass away." These are some of the crucial wisdoms of hope, the kind of hope which time and again has proven itself to be as vital to the human spirit as oxygen, and as fortifying and fructifying.

Such hope is an irreplaceable ingredient of the first of the three P's of healthy humanness: Perspective, Proportion and Pacing. Perspective puts each individual episode of existence in a larger, meaningful framework. It keeps the pieces, especially the disappointing pieces, from swelling hopelessly out of size and blocking the channels of growth.

As a baby, a cousin of mine was once playing on the floor near my foot. He suddenly focused his eyes on the mysterious entity of my shoe, which was keeping time with some music. All at once terror seized the child, and I could sense that he was experiencing my foot as a strange, threatening and disembodied reality. He was seeing it out of perspective, just as many people view sexuality, for instance, out of perspective and in a depersonalized setting, and hence find it a source of terror on the one hand, or of irresistible fascination on the other.

In addition to perspective, which relates to the broad picture of meaning within which a man locates separate elements, a person needs a sense of proportion in his response to the demands of reality. It is not enough for a good cook to mix the proper ingredients for a successful cake. The parts must be mixed in due proportion. Likewise, a man needs balance in the diet of the activities and goals which comprise his life style.

This diet will vary according to each person's talents, needs and circumstances. Figuring out the best proportion will be to a great extent a matter of trial and error. The proof of the pudding will lie in the

137

degree of creative and humane productivity character-
izing a man's daily existence. Here a man has to learn
to listen to a deep, inner voice of rightness or wrong-
ness which will tell him, at once or gradually, whether
he is doing his part to fulfill his destiny as a human
being.

Pacing is the third element of wholesome living.
Men are creatures of time, of slow unfoldings and
piecemeal progressions. Like the shepherd who should
be at the head of his flock, but not a mile ahead, a man
needs to lead his energies forward in some orderly
formation if he is to preserve his psychic unity.
Better to go slow on the right road, warned St. Augustine, than fast on the wrong one. At issue here is a
man's humility, his willingess to be what he is and
do what he reasonably can. There is no fixed rule for
everyone in this matter, but a man will be well advised to check his pacing, especially if his activities
are causing some noisy wrenching within himself or
around himself. Internal sputterings, on the other
hand, or honking of nearby horns could be a signal
that he is frittering away his energies in laziness or
triviality.

Those people honking their horns may, of course,
just be impatient people with their own pacing problems. After a reasonable point, there is no sense in
bothering much about the opinion of others. Take
refuge in this pleasantly cynical thought: You
wouldn't worry what others thought about you, if you
knew how seldom they do.

One of the rewards of self-knowledge, which will
invariably bring you a sharper view of your own
flaws, inconsistencies and clay feet, is that it can brace
you to endure more graciously the faults of the man
next door. Such is the wit and wisdom of W. H.
Auden's words: "Love your crooked neighbor with

your crooked heart."

In any case, the business of loving remains the central task of the human heart. This truth becomes more vital as it becomes more difficult in a pressurized age like our own. The reason for this vitalness is suggested by the inscription to be found on one of those wall posters which have grown so popular over the last few years, especially among students. It reads: "Nothing makes sense until you love somebody."

It is essential for something to make sense if a man is to respond wholesomely to the pressures of existence. More than that, a feeling of senselessness will only multiply and magnify the frustrating pressures of existence. The philosopher Nietzsche noted pertinently that a man can endure almost any *how* if he has a *why*.

This sense of why, of meaning and purpose and value in one's life, is one of the most precious assets of the Christian or of any man wholeheartedly dedicated to some value seen as ultimate and objective. Viktor Frankl, a European psychotherapist who as a prisoner in a Nazi concentration camp learned the meaning of meaning, has given renewed currency in recent years to the idea of meaning, especially in his well-known *Man's Search for Meaning*. Frankl sees the spiritual dimension in man as man's unique and distinctive attribute. He finds this dimension irreducible, that is, he doesn't see it merely as a function which can be reduced or traced back to some lower biological or physical level, however much it may be linked with these levels in its present mode of operation.

Frankl regards consciousness and responsibility as the two qualities of man's spiritual dimension. The drive which man experiences to respond to value is part of his very nature, and he can be sick spiritually without being sick in a clinical, psychiatric sense.

Frankl's name for the type of therapy needed to cure men of the disease of senselessness in their lives is "logotherapy," that is, "healing" by the rediscovery of "meaning."

Such meaning is to be found in three kinds of values: 1) creative ones, which lead a man to act; 2) experiential values, which prompt a man to undergo such experiences as beauty and love; and 3) attitudinal values, which a man adopts in the face of situations which are out of his control. In this last case, a man can achieve his sublimest moral grandeur and his fullest humanity by the posture of soul he takes toward realities such as an incurable disease and death itself.

Genuine human response to real values, despite the pressures to become unreal and inhuman: This has been the theme of these chapters. A man is as great as the real values which stretch him. It is never too early to begin being real, and never too late to start. Viewed (in the words of Adrian van Kaam) as a mystery to be lived rather than as a problem to be solved, life will provide the answers to its own questions, though not necessarily in the form we are expecting.

Because we have preconceived expectations, we are often unconsciously battling against the divine pattern of destiny in our lives. The Greek writer Nikos Kazantzakis tells an arresting story in his book *Report from Greco*. Visiting a saintly and ascetic monk on a remote island, the author asked him:

"Do you still wrestle with the devil, Father Makarios?"

"Not any longer, my child. I have grown old, and he has grown old with me. He doesn't have the strength . . . I wrestle with God."

"With God!" I exclaimed with astonishment. "And you hope to win?"

"I hope to lose, my child."

A monk of our own times, who did some lovely losing in his lifelong search for values, may be appropriately invoked to speak the final words of this series on the pressurized Christian. Wrote Thomas Merton:

"Anxiety is inevitable in an age of crisis like ours. Don't make it worse by deceiving yourself and acting as if you were immune to all inner trepidation. God does not ask you not to feel anxious—but to trust Him no matter how you feel." ●

Man needs to keep noticing people and things in their uniqueness if he is to stay as alive as possible to the real world.

a play...

Once Upon a Timeless

In the chapter on "Wonder and Delight," I stressed a man's need to keep noticing people and things in their uniqueness if he is to stay as alive as possible to the real world. The contrary bad habit is to lump people and things together into general categories.

Some years ago I wrote the following "play" as an illustration of these two different approaches and in an effort to promote the first approach in any possible reader or audience.

As is widely known, the philosopher Plato tended to regard the everyday world as a kind of illusion. For him, the real world was the unseen world of pure, eternal ideas. This play, *Once Upon a Timeless*, is playfully set in a quasi-Platonic world of disembodied thoughts and ideas.

Though it is, at best, a "closet" drama meant more to be read than acted, it was twice presented appreciatively in Baltimore's Old St. Mary's Seminary chapel. The Judge spoke from a balcony behind the

143

audience. The other characters, dressed toga-style, spoke their lines before the audience. Apart from a bluish spotlight and the atmospheric glow of several candles, the chapel was dark.

Time: None, but not never
Place: None, but not nowhere

* * *

JUDGE SOBERTHOUGHT: Order in the court! Order in the court! Everyone please settle down and stop thinking. This confusion is enough to put a Thought out of its mind.

SIR GRIMTHOUGHT: Are you ready to have the two defendants brought in, Sir?

SOBERTHOUGHT: Yes, at once. Just how long do you expect eternity to last?

SIR FORETHOUGHT: Happy Eternity, Judge Soberthought!

SIR AFTERTHOUGHT: I concur stoutly in that worthy wish, Your Honor.

SOBERTHOUGHT: That is all very well. But I want to warn you two that anything you think may be held against you.

SIR PLEADINGTHOUGHT: May I have a thought with you, Sir?

JUDGE: Think on, Sir Pleadingthought.

PLEADINGTHOUGHT: Well, Sir, if I may state the point baldly, Your Honor, I am here to defend Sir Forethought and Sir Afterthought, Your Honor.

PART OF THE CROWD: Hurrah! Hurrah!

JUDGE: Here! Here! This unseemly demonstration ill befits the solemn nature of this case.

GRIMTHOUGHT: And I, Your Honor, am here to represent the State in prosecuting these two rotten Ideas.

PART OF THE CROWD: Bravo! Bravo!

JUDGE: Come, come! You may continue, Sir Grimthought.

GRIMTHOUGHT: Thank you, Sir. Inasmuch as the nefarious fabrications, falsehoods and frauds of the two defendants here present are only too well known to any thinking Thought to need further proof, I submit that Your Honor is entitled to sentence them at once.

JUDGE: What think the three members of the jury about this proposal?

SIR RANDOMTHOUGHT: I can only think for myself, Your Honor, but I am not at all convinced that what Sirs Fore- and Afterthought maintain is altogether gratuitous, not to say fatuous. To put it bluntly, I must confess to a nowise negligible sentiment of reluctance in affirming the certitude of what may indeed turn out to be nothing but a deceptive conjecture, precipitously embraced. That, Your Honor, is the long-short of my position on the subject.

JUDGE: It certainly is. How about you, Sir Straddlethought? Think up!

145

SIR STRADDLETHOUGHT: Well, Your Honor, I at least can be more definitive. I have given the testimony of all parties careful consideration. I have investigated the private thought-lives of everyone concerned. I have consulted eminent Learned-Thoughts and hence I am prepared to assert with unqualified firmness and unflinching courage that I cannot make up my mind one way or the other.

JUDGE: Well thought out! And how about you, Sir Happythought?

SIR HAPPYTHOUGHT: Pardon me, Judge, but I am little hard of thinking. Would you repeat your question?

JUDGE: *I asked, how about you?*

HAPPYTHOUGHT: Just fine and dandy, thank you. How about yourself?

JUDGE: *No, no. I was soliciting an expression of your opinion about the guilt of these two defendants.*

HAPPYTHOUGHT: Oh, pardon me! Truth to tell, Your Honor, I am not at all clear about this whole melancholy affair. Whenever I come upon my fellow Thoughts discussing these strange goings-on, I can't grasp the main points for all the arguing and shouting.

JUDGE: Well, that leaves us with only 13 possibilities and nine probabilities. But I have an idea—somewhat unorthodox, you may fancy, but not altogether illegal. We'll let the defendants think for themselves.

FORETHOUGHT: We thank you, Your Honor, from the lowest depths of our minds.

JUDGE: Well, now is your chance.

FORETHOUGHT: You see, Your Honor, it all started this way, so to think. Afterthought and I had grown considerably bored with life here in the Kingdom of Thought. Sitting around all the timeless, doing nothing but entertaining ideas had lost its pristine appeal and didn't seem so ideal anymore. After an endless struggle, we finally yielded to temptation and dared to trespass into the forbidden territory of Brinkthought.

JUDGE: Is that the truth, Afterthought?

AFTERTHOUGHT: If not precisely, Your Honor, it is a rational facsimile thereof.

FORE: We tried to persuade ourselves that the inevitable wouldn't happen to us. But it did.

AFTER: Yes, Your Honor. We finally fell over the Brink, tumbled backwards through 212 degrees of abstraction, and landed in the Kingdom of Time-Space, which our legends and fairy tales tell about.

GRIMTHOUGHT: That's a lie, Your Honor! Any Idea which would have fallen that low would surely have been squelched.

FORE: But, Your Honor. That's just it. Luck was with us, and we landed smack in the middle of the head of an open-minded student.

AFTER: Exactly, Your Honor. And inasmuch as it was summertime, the student's mind was practically unoccupied.

FORE: And inasmuch as it was this particular student's

147

mind, there was a certain friendly softness in the center where we hit.

STRADDLETHOUGHT: There has been many a thoughtless Thought who has fallen over the Brink, but none has ever returned.

GRIMTHOUGHT: Exactly, Your Honor. Some member from practically every family of Ideas has been irretrievably lost that way at one timeless or another.

JUDGE: I need no reminder on that topic. Why, it has been only a few ages since a whole mindful of the tribe of Treeness plunged over the Brink.

HAPPYTHOUGHT: Out of mind, out of sight, as the old saying goes.

PLEADINGTHOUGHT: Please, Your Honor, give my clients a chance to explain.

JUDGE: Go on.

FORE: Well, Sir, not to change the subject, but we have plenty we could tell about those Treethoughts.

VOICE FROM THE AUDIENCE: Oh, my lost Thoughts, my little lost Thoughts!

JUDGE: Please, Mrs. Pinetreeness, try to contain yourself!

AFTER: I trust this revelation will grieve no one unduly, but we saw countless other lost Thoughts.

EVERYONE IN THE AUDIENCE: Oh, our wandering Thoughts!

JUDGE: Here! Here! No wonder you both have been charged with disturbing the peace, you two exciting Ideas.

FORE: We meant no harm. It's the veriest truth, Your Honor. We did see Treeness and Loveliness and Skyness and Songness, only they were all tangled up in, in . . . .

AFTER: In, in . . . .

JUDGE: Well, out with it! All tangled up in what?

FORE: I scarcely know how to phrase it, Your Honor. I mean to say they were all splendidly stuck in what they call *"matter."*

GRIMTHOUGHT: There they go again with that accursed double-Thought!

JUDGE: Now, my good Grimthought, don't take the matter too seriously.

GRIMTHOUGHT: On the contrary, most worthy Judge, I insist that this matter cannot be taken too seriously. Just wait and see what superstitious mummery these two fakers will weave from the *harmless* notion of matter.

PLEADINGTHOUGHT: Please, Your Honor, give my clients a chance to explain.

JUDGE: Go on.

AFTER: The fact is, Sir, that the very student we fell in with was himself a flickering sort of Idea.

149

FORE: Only, he had a body on.

JUDGE: A what?

FORE: A body, Your Honor.

GRIMTHOUGHT: Your Honor, I protest. This trial has fallen to a new low, an all-timeless low. The very thought of a Thought going around with a body on! It's indecent, Sir.

JUDGE: I must confess that I am not absolutely sure what this controversial body is.

AFTER: Bodies can't be all that bad, Your Honor. In fact, most of the people we saw seemed to be rather pleasantly attached to them.

GRIMTHOUGHT: There they go again with that double-Thought. Your Honor, I wager that nobody here, pardon me, I mean, no *one* here understands the meaning of words like "body" or "people" or "student." Everyone is just too high-minded to admit the fact. We are letting these imposters fool us.

JUDGE: My, my. This is most Thought-provoking. I perceive that we must have some definitions.

GRIMTHOUGHT: I am happy to point out, Your Honor, that definitions won't be needed. These two scoundrels have yet to explain how they could possibly have gotten back into Thoughtdom, even if their lies were true.

PLEADINGTHOUGHT: Please, Your Honor. Give my clients a chance to explain.

150

JUDGE: Go on.

FORE: Most happily, Your Honor, Afterthought and I were having an unbelievable time of it, providing you know what time is. We sat, each on one side of our student's longitudinal fissure, providing you know what *that* is. We each had one eye to see Time-Space out of, and one ear to eavesdrop through.

AFTER: And it was a world of unearthly beauty that we found. Your Honor, you have no idea how the Thought of Dawn and Sun and Snow look like when they get all entangled with matter and mingle together in a haphazard charm.

FORE: And if you could once witness a sunrise, when the sun is a wandering blister of blood that fevers up the sky.

JUDGE: Now you're getting poetical.

FORE: That's true, Your Honor. But the earth is so infected with loveliness that you can't think about it without breaking out into a rash of poetry.

AFTER: And we saw it all, with his own two eyes.

GRIMTHOUGHT: Once again, I must protest. These two poetizers have yet to explain how they could have gotten back into Thoughtdom.

AFTER: Actually, it was very simple. As soon as school began, our student's mind began getting so crowded with educational things—like telephone numbers, football signals and dates for dances—that Forethought and I started getting more and more abstracted in his

151

mind until we finally managed to boost ourselves back across the Brink.

GRIMTHOUGHT: That's preposterous! Though, I must admit, no more so than the other intoxicated stories they have been spreading about that fictitious place called "the world"—

> Their universe is an improbable place. It's not a
> bit likely at all.
> The stories I've heard are mad and absurd. Such
> tales are too taxingly tall.
> I really can't see what use there could be for
> things like a moon or a star. And if such
> things, *et cetera,* have no *raison d'être,* it
> simply can't be that they are.
> I can't help but grin when they speak of the spin
> of the earth in its aerial orbit.
> Since I can't conceive it, how could I believe it?
> I never could hope to absorb it.

JUDGE: That's what I call fighting fire with fire, poetically speaking.

PLEADINGTHOUGHT: Your Honor, on behalf of my clients, I must insist that they be given a chance to explain what they saw. I am sure that the jury will be persuaded that my clients are not fantasizing, but tell what they truly saw, I suppose.

JUDGE: All right, then. Suppose you two describe some of the more remarkable things you saw on your alleged journey.

FORE: Gladly, Your Honor. I think that, next to man himself, the most amazing things in the universe are sunsets and stars, flowers and birds and jewels.

AFTER: And next to man himself I most marveled at the ocean and snow, grass and storms and music.

JUDGE: I am quite bewildered. I know what Starness and Snowness and Grassness are, but from the way you two talk, these Ideas must somehow become more entrancing when the earth gets a hold of them.

AFTER: Ah, worthy Judge, a little bit of matter makes a world of difference. It provides you with the delightful terror of thunderstorms and, afterwards, with the gradual, reluctant rumblings that growl on the fringe of the fury.

FORE: And flowers, which are tints and fragrances merged together, simmering, and sweetly angering to a boil of beauty. And, if you are a man, you get stars too.

JUDGE: And what are stars?

FORE: Oh, stars are pinches of frosted dazzle sent to season the night and its scary black.

AFTER: And you get hailstones, which are winter's splinters, made out of frozen fire that crackles at the windowpanes of cozy cottages. Hail is a sort of over-anxious snow—and snow is like the chips and fragments of some shattered vanilla silence.

AFTER: And, Your Honor, you can't conceive how pleasantly cool green grass tastes to the eyes.

JUDGE: Eyes? And what are those?

153

AFTER: Men have them to savor the shapes and colors of the world with. I remember one pair I saw. They were like two chocolates, darkly dazzling and brightly fevered. I think they would have melted, only they were embedded in two diamonds of snow called the whites of the eyes.

FORE: And I saw a pair of lover's eyes, all enthralled and quite out of breath, stuttering as they tried to speak.

HAPPYTHOUGHT: Pardon me, Sirs, but I can no longer restrain a curiosity which your recital has aroused. You both selected wonderful things to tell us about, and you both began by saying, "Next to man himself." Just what exactly does this being a man involve?

FORE: I was afraid someone was going to ask that! The trouble is, man is so unbelievable and mysterious that it would be an agony to try to depict him.

AFTER: That is correct, Sir Happythought. For man is a fantastic fabric of yeses, noes and in-betweens; an intolerable brilliance shot weirdly through with shadows and insanities. He is a salad of absurdities, an epic, a jingle, a hieroglyph—the loveliest, loneliest pilgrim on his planet. . . .

FORE: He's an architect of visions, a leveler of cities, a lie, a dream, a savage softness, whose only simile is another man, whose only parallel is a paradox, unwondering wonder of the universe.

HAPPYTHOUGHT: Unwondering?

FORE: Yes, Sir. Strange to say, most men soon get over

154

the shock of being alive and aware in such an incredible state of affairs as is the universe.

AFTER: But there are a few things which usually molest the monotony they lapse into—like babies, for instance, and falling in love.

JUDGE: Would you mind elaborating a little?

AFTER: Not at all. It seems that two human beings keep company awhile, and the next thing you know, there are three of them. It is quite irregular mathematically, but it is clever economics and excellent poetry—since the third human being is quite dependably a very little fellow and decidedly helpless. He is so helpless at first that his mother and father are forced to pay attention. And this close attention almost never fails to rekindle their sense of wonder.

FORE: Yes, Your Honor, babies are an admirable invention. I remember even composing a poem on earth about them. It went something like:

> A baby, all his seeing spent in tiny, total wonderment;
> A baby feeling slightly the worse for stumbling on the universe,
> And still unused to many a feature about the task of being a creature;
> A guest who has to learn as yet the rules of cosmic etiquette.

HAPPYTHOUGHT: Is there anything else that makes men sometimes wonder?

AFTER: Yes, a very sad thing. It is called death.

155

Nobody knows exactly what it is. But death is like a sudden winter that unheats the flesh of man, a clammy gust that snuffs the rowdy flicker from his eyes, and molds him into a terrible muteness. It stanches all the gorgeous bleed of rapture from his voice. It freezes him into a most stubborn fixity. You ply his soldered ears with all your persuasions; you plead the most imperious claims of blood and love, but no solitary spark responds to all your frantic frictioning.

JUDGE: That sounds very sad indeed. But I think you two have now had the opportunity to present your case before the court. The jury may now retire to consult and discuss the guilt or innocence of the two defendants. While we are waiting perhaps you two would oblige us with a further description of this confusing notion of a body, which you mentioned earlier.

FORE: Most happily, Your Honor:

> Since man is called upon to be more than mere gelatin,
> He makes no bones about the need for a skeleton.

AFTER: And having often to twist, turn, toss and tussle, He makes regular use of both loose and stringent muscle.

FORE: Another device which he presses into service Is a system which is generally referred to as nervous.

AFTER: And since six quarts of blood are the juice of his battery, It is not in vain that one of his systems is circu látory.

FORE: Moreover, it being in the long run better never to be, as it were, out of breath, Respiration by no means artificially preserves him from death.

AFTER: Nor must we omit to make mention of his digestive apparatus. Especially since no other system is normally kept half so busy as that is.

FORE: Taking more within himself than he can store without inflation, Man discovers what he can do without, by a process of elimination.

AFTER: A final system about which much opinion seems errant Is the reproductive one, whose goal should be a-parent.

JUDGE: That may be all very interesting, but it sounds so complicated that it must be quite bothersome to be a man.

AFTER: Oh, no, Your Honor. I hope that no one will accuse me of lacking patriotism, but I'd give anything to be a man:
I wish I were a man, could do the things he can—
Could raise my eyes and scan the sky's tantalizing span.
Just to splash my face with sun, rinse my breath with crispy air,
Let refreshing raindrops run with cooling footsteps through my hair;
Even pain and death were worth a single year upon the earth.
I wish I were a man.

FORE: To savor shower-droplets flung upon my lips and barren tongue;

157

To have some gracious vision burst on eyes long
parched with beauty-thirst;
Even pain and death were worth a single month upon
the earth.
I wish I were a man.

AFTER: To feel the yield of sodden sand beneath my
wandering feet;
To scoop decaying foam in hand, or taste some bitter-
sweet;
Even pain and death were worth a single day upon the
earth.
I wish I were a man.

FORE: Could I but deserve on the way that I'd wend
Some one fellow creature to love and befriend;
Could he but respond with a glad, total heart
Before we must journey forever apart;
Even pain and death were worth that magic moment
on the earth;

FORE AND AFTER: We wish we were a man.

GRIMTHOUGHT: Your Honor, it is well that the jury
is in consultation, or I should feel obliged to object to
this maudlin appeal to the emotions of the court. These
versifiers are trying to make us Ideas take on a different coloring.

JUDGE: Well, I see that the jury is reentering. We shall
soon know what fate awaits the defendants. Sir
Randomthought, acquaint us with your decision.

RANDOMTHOUGHT: Your Honor, I shall be brief, as
usual. This whole tale is outlandish. Man is nothing
but a figment of the imagination, a reactionary super-

158

stition. The Kingdom of Thoughtdom has managed to get along very agreeably without the intrusion of this dangerous notion. I cast my vote against these two rabble-rousers.

JUDGE: And you, Sir Straddlethought?

STRADDLETHOUGHT: Your Honor, believe it or not, I find myself siding with the two defendants. Their earnestness persuades me. And their story is so fantastic that I can't imagine anyone inventing it.

JUDGE: Well, that leaves us undecided. Sir Happythought, it seems that everything depends on you.

HAPPYTHOUGHT: Your Honor, it is with extreme difficulty that I announce my decision. I, too, was greatly repelled by the outrageous incredibility of the universe as depicted by the defendants. Watching them closely, however, I was much impressed by their seeming sincerity. I found myself willing to allow that such miracles might happen. After all, planets that spin around all the time at untidy intervals from the so-called sun may be silly but they are not entirely impossible. It is also true that many of our legends and myths tell of creatures like man, but maybe that is just a coincidence. Then, too, this talk about rain that conveniently waters the earth so that flowers can grow—maybe this is mere wish fulfillment, and maybe it isn't.

So, more and more, I grew ready to accept the two defendants as telling the truth. Indeed, I was all prepared to vote for them, when they made one statement which ruined everything.

JUDGE: And what was that, my dear Happythought?

HAPPYTHOUGHT: It was when they said . . . when they said that all men do not wonder all the time at all the things in the world. That I could never believe, if the world and man are both true. That would be the most monstrous impossibility that was ever thought of. So I must vote against them. They are guilty of fraud!

JUDGE: It is then, Sirs Forethought and Afterthought, my solemn duty to sentence you both to eternal exile. You will be taken and thrown over the Brink of Thoughtdom. Have you any final remarks to make?

FORE: Yes, Your Honor. We are both delighted at our punishment. Since we returned and began telling our story, the Brink has been so closely guarded that we feared we should never be able to return to the world.

AFTER: Now, you have saved us. We who are about to live salute you. We only hope that when we arrive back in the world we will find some minds open enough to harbor us, a couple of wandering, wondering Thoughts.

THE END